OPEN

Big Lessons in Small Retail and Living the Shopkeeper Dream

Ana Maria Muñoz

OPEN: *Big Lessons in Small Retail and Living the Shopkeeper Dream*

Copyright © 2024 Ana Maria Muñoz

All rights reserved. If you feel compelled to share any part of this book for review purposes, thank you for giving credit to the author.

The scanning, uploading, re-printing and distribution of this book without permission is a theft of the author's intellectual property. Please contact the author for written permission.

The events and conversations in this book have been written to the best of the author's ability, although some names and details have been changed to protect the privacy of individuals.

Design by Tess McCabe ~ tessmccabe.com.au

ISBN 9780645963915 (paperback)
ISBN 9780645963939 (hardback)

First Edition

Published by Lucky We Publishing

For my family who opens my heart and world every day.

CONTENTS

Letter to the reader   1

PART I: THE DREAM IS PERSONAL   7
The Dream   8
Raleigh, the Port of Call   19
My Why   22
Launching the Store   27
Burning Out   32
Getting the Spark Back   36

PART II: PREPPING THE SHOPKEEPER   43
Tackling the Proverbial Toolbox   44
Take Personal Inventory   48
Make Money Your Best Friend   58
Plan to Pay Yourself ASAP   63
Anticipate Your Commercial + Community Ecosystem   68
Own Your Shopkeeper Title   74

PART III: PREPPING THE STORE   79
Choose Your Location   80
Build Out the Dream   85
Pay, Ask, Give   91
Set It and (Don't) Forget It   96
Buy Your Opening Inventory   102

PART IV: OPENING   107
Celebrate!   108
Count on Community   110
Finding Your People   113
Mind Your Energy   117
Show Up for Your Team   122

PART V: OPERATING   125
Creating the In-Store Experience   126
Please Press Play   131
Be of Service Online   134
Lift All [Brands] Boats   139
Maintain Your Merchandise Mojo   144
What Else Can You Serve?   148
Sell Your Own Products   153
Trade In Trust   157
Sharing, Not Selling   160
Get Noticed   165
Pay to Get Noticed   169
Be Cool and Collaborate   173
Express Your Gratitude   176
Consider the Conscious Customer   180
Good Intentions   188

PART VI: ONWARD   193
Learning to Take Personal Inventory   194
Reframing the Journey   206
How's the Fit?   209
Which Road Will You Take?   214

Afterword   223
Acknowledgments   225
Resources   227

LETTER TO THE READER

You have the Shopkeeper Dream for a reason, but there's a lot to unpack before launching your dream business. And I'm not just talking about boxes full of merchandise.

Between professional experiences in retail and a personal passion, I was well suited to be a Shopkeeper. I loved retail, and I knew retail, but what I didn't know well enough before jumping into my dream and launching my shop was *myself*. Doing your best work requires knowing yourself intimately—how you operate and the conditions you need to thrive. And after five years of shopkeeping, and subsequently closing my brick-and-mortar and e-commerce store, I recognized that when I opened my store, I unknowingly opened myself up to immense personal growth.

Owning and operating a retail store was not my ultimate calling, but it taught me my greatest lesson: how to take personal inventory. Taking personal inventory is intentionally checking in with yourself to ensure that your professional and personal lives align. To do so, you must dig into the depths of your "Personal Backroom" to take stock of what's missing, what's off, and what's spot on. From your personality to your deepest fears and desires, taking personal inventory often and honestly can make a huge difference in how you launch, grow, and evolve your dream. The practice clarifies what decisions you're about to make and what steps you've already taken. The clearer you are, the more buoyant you can be in your business operations and personal well-being. And being well through it all is the goal. I was unaware of this notion when I launched and grew my store, but I would not be who I am today—and who I will become—without the experiences and lessons that came from chasing energetic sparks and saying YES to my retail dream.

The five years I ran my store, Port of Raleigh, were full of fun, beauty, and community. I created what I wanted to see in the world and became a version of myself that I long fantasized about. I got to play with my strengths while helping people bring more intention and joy into their homes and everyday lives.

Of course, some days knocked me down. There were days when I didn't check my personal energies and struggled to be present, days when I was not in the best mindset to get the results I envisioned for my store and in my personal life. I got in my own way and struggled as a new mom and business owner more than I needed to. As with any entrepreneurial pursuit, I was challenged in more ways than I anticipated. I felt extremely vulnerable and often questioned my decisions. I felt totally in control while equally out of control. There were days when I knew I was right where I was meant to be—flowing and flying high—and others when I was pushing boulders uphill, wondering what had become of my life. Through it all, I did my best to nurture my dream with the awareness I had at any given moment. Even when I couldn't see or feel it, I was rewarded for my efforts.

When I started the store, my vision of success meant reaching the operational dream: a full-time team to manage the daily tasks of running the store while I focused on buying merchandise, marketing to the community, and other creative and visionary projects. The business would be profitable by year three, and I'd pay myself with increases year after year. I'd also have all the flex time I wanted to travel and be with my family.

Nearly five years in, I had not achieved the full-time operations team. I still didn't have the time I wanted with my family, and I was definitely not paying myself as hoped. Our growth trajectory projected that the store's net profits would have kicked in after our fifth anniversary, but our fifth and final year was 2020. After the roller coaster of COVID-19 lockdowns that began in March of that year, success meant closing the business without debt, showing gratitude to our loyal customers, and creating time and space for the lifestyle my family and I wanted next.

Creating and closing Port of Raleigh (PofR) reframed my vision for success. I was successful because I put my vision out there, took risks, and created a community. I faced external and internal challenges that deepened my skill set and my sense of self. I learned lessons that will remain with me no matter where life takes me. The store was successful because it created value for the community it served.

Despite the satisfaction I felt when I hung up my Shopkeeper hat for good, I knew this to be true: Had I known to dig deep into my Personal Backroom and explore the complete picture of what I wanted for my life and for the store, what I call my "heartset," from the onset, I could have experienced my time as a brick-and-mortar retail entrepreneur—and mom, boss, buyer, merchandiser, marketer, bookkeeper, online store administrator, photographer, social media manager, shipper, janitor, wife, sister, daughter, friend, and member of the community—more joyfully and driven the business more effectively to reach my initial metrics of success. Also true: I knew I had to share this knowledge.

Like many of you, I sought to know more about opening a store through how-to books and online articles with practical checklists. With two decades of experience in retail and my passion for design and creating joyful experiences, the Shopkeeper Dream was a reality. I led myself to believe that my relevant skill sets made this venture a slam dunk for success. So to every questionnaire that asked whether or not I had what it took to be an entrepreneur, I answered with a full-bodied "YES!"

However, those yes-or-no questionnaires, pragmatic bullet-point checklists, and work resumes only scratch the surface of what it means to be a Shopkeeper. I needed something deeper and more relatable that took my particular season of life into account. I needed to read honest stories and hear firsthand accounts grounded in authentic experiences, not hypotheticals or detached examples of what could be. In my research, I didn't find a checklist for my heartset—a guide that showed me I could get into and consistently remain in a healthy, productive, and thriving mindset. Nothing I read prepared me for how emotionally challenging the Shopkeeper lifestyle would be as a new mom and clueless introvert. That's why we're here now. You are reading these words and hearing me spilling my soul because I want you to know you don't have to operate from a dark and cluttered Personal Backroom in *any* season of life. Being a Shopkeeper can feel like a lonely endeavor, like every problem falls to you to solve. But you are not alone, and there are tools within reach.

To assist you with taking personal inventory, this book includes considerations to help you craft a vision for your store that includes the most important element: *you*. Whether you're looking at your first location or considering your third, it's key that you're honest with yourself about your goals, hopes, fears, and what your life will be like at every step of the journey. If you want to paint a picture, it's best to know what you're painting and the tools and materials that are available to you.

Too many how-to books and retail experts focus on utilitarian checklists while matters of the heart are cliff-noted or left out altogether. That's why I wrote this book. I want to help you paint a better picture. *OPEN* is the book I wish I'd read before opening my dream store (and reread throughout my time operating and eventually closing my dream store). The intention is less how-to *build* and more how-to *be* because being true to your truest self can be the hardest thing to do.

You have the Shopkeeper Dream for a reason, and I hope that my story, insights, and the lessons I learned along the way serve as a helpful guide as you bring your dream to life with less friction and a whole lot more joy. From the sales floor to the soul, I address the practical elements of building your business, focusing on the energies and purpose of the Shopkeeper Dream while giving it space to grow, thrive, and evolve. My wins can be your wins too. And my failures, for lack of a better word, can be avoided.

As you build your business and create retail experiences for others to enjoy, or if you're daydreaming about doing so one day, keep your personal inventory list close, and remember that the

Shopkeeper Dream is yours to shape. Your present and future are wide open.

Not a Shopkeeper? Welcome. I invite you to peek behind the cash wrap and step into the backroom. Perhaps a story or two from my experience as a Shopkeeper will resonate with your own entrepreneurial journey, inform on the commercial + community ecosystem we're all a part of, or remind you of a special Shopkeeper in your life.

PART I
THE DREAM IS PERSONAL

THE DREAM

The Shopkeeper Dream is a desire to share what you're passionate about by creating a physical place where these passions can delight others, and the objects you curate are celebrated through a common connection. This shared physical place benefits your customers and community, and personally fulfills you creatively and professionally.

It can sound romantic and even magical, but this dream, this place you envision, is also an inventory-based business that requires a delicate balance of being financially guided without clouding your passion.

I know the Shopkeeper Dream *very* well.

Port of Raleigh wasn't my first business or stint in retail, but it was my first time playing big. Big because of what I was willing to risk, put into it, and hope to get out of it in return. Big because it would be out in the public realm for all to see and experience in real time. I embraced the challenges and general unknowns of setting up shop—hard work didn't faze me, and I was too excited about all the positive possibilities. I've been entranced by retail for a lifetime. Not pursuing this dream would lead to regret, and I've never wanted to regret things in life.

I lost track of how many people asked me about my dream with questions like, "What's your background/story/reason for opening the store or moving to Raleigh?" PofR was unlike any other store in town, and I took such inquiries as a compliment. Their interest in my background was due to their interest in the store itself. My default response became, "I've lived all over the world and have always wanted to have a store to showcase the designs and products that I have loved along the way. The time and place finally felt right to go for it." From that point, the conversation would evolve depending on how curious and conversational the person was. People would often open up about their travels, past homes, and shared passions. I was always open about my story and happy to share it because every detail in my response gave context for the physical space we stood in at that moment and the items on the shelves.

Context builds connection, so before we get to the prepping, opening, operating, and onward stages of the Shopkeeper Dream (and related personal stories), let's start with my background and the context for my dream, how I brought it to life, and what led to discovering the power of taking personal inventory. In other words, what inspired me to pursue the Dream and open PofR? What was living the Shopkeeper Dream like for me and why?

Ana Maria's Clothes Shop was the first retail experience I designed. I was in fourth grade, and my carefully constructed too-small-for-Barbie yet too-big-for-Lego storefront was my contribution to my class's California Gold Rush town. The shop was made of tough particle board my dad hand-sawed to my specifications. It featured doll-house-size touches like gold door hinges and snap buttons as doorknobs. The period-appropriate fashions that I drew and displayed in the cellophane-covered windows were the real pride of the place. Playing Shopkeeper by envisioning, designing, and sharing the results with the world, aka my fellow ten-year-olds, was a creative exercise that left a big imprint.

In college, I leaped toward the future with a business plan for an e-commerce store. My fashion merchandising classmates and I were tasked with starting our own boutique store, and I was the only student to present an online business. It was 2007, and I'll never forget standing in front of my peers, proudly presenting wireframes and mocked-up web pages for my digital storefront while they looked at me like I was from another planet. They weren't just confused because my storefront would be displayed as web pages on a computer monitor. My apparel was from emerging and independent sustainable clothing brands. E-commerce was in its infancy at the time, and sustainable fashion had a reputation of being "crunchy" and "granola." I wanted to help change that perception and narrative through e-commerce, starting with ten or so modern brands that aligned with my mission. Despite being the odd woman out in class that day, my niche concept felt important and exciting.

I felt a sense of accomplishment in choosing a unique direction for my boutique project. Creating something from nothing and taking on the challenge of envisioning and crafting a new concept, even if only on paper, was thrilling. It was the first time I created a brand from beginning to end, digging deep to discover and determine everything from philosophical purpose to operational details and marketing tactics.

I worked in fashion and retail throughout most of my college career. During the first two years, I worked at Nordstrom and became an assistant manager in the Juniors Department, named BP, short for Brass Plum. I was first offered a job at GAP, but Nordstrom won me over with its excellent customer service, delicious bistro and cafe, and commission-based pay. I completed my last two undergrad years with internships at a boutique fashion PR firm, a fashion trend forecasting agency, and a Hollywood celebrity-focused marketing group. I learned how clothing brands and media collided. I swam in the ecosystem and timelines from clothing production to sales floor readiness and saw first-hand how brand experiences could be enhanced with highly strategic placements and partnerships. By graduation, I'd managed to play, learn, and earn money in the multifaceted world of retail. Each experience gave me confidence—and the opportunity to see the bigger retail picture while tending to the details.

Right after college, I landed an internship with TOMS Shoes in its early days. I was hired full time to coordinate and ultimately manage the giving side, as we called it, of the revolutionary One for One for-profit business model. At age twenty-three, my job took me to Argentina, Ethiopia, South Africa, and parts of the US I had never been. I felt lucky I had the opportunity be in the communities with the people we were working for. My day-to-day was working for the good of others, and the people I worked alongside were inspiring. But what drew me to the company wasn't just its One for One mission: they were doing good deeds through fashion, retail, and brilliant marketing. It was all initially very exciting for me. But my scope of work didn't play in fashion, retail, or marketing. I was ultimately swimming in

Non-Government Organization (NGO), Request for Proposal (RFPs), and spreadsheets for tracking our efforts in giving shoes to people around the world. I yearned to feel creatively engaged. My friends on the creative team would often catch me looking over their shoulders at their graphic design projects. Or they would see me hovering by their wall-mounted visual boards for the next season's collection or campaign. I wanted to hang out with the design stuff, or with the marketing team planning the campaigns, events, and retail launches.

TOMS was a fast-growing company, and my stress levels reflected the long hours and required energy input. Acne began to show on my face like never before, and I was developing carpal tunnel syndrome with joint pain in my fingers that got so bad, it was difficult to brush my teeth or hold the steering wheel.

It wasn't just work-related stress that manifested itself. I had started making handbags out of vintage scarves and assembling jewelry at home in the evenings and weekends, which required a lot of dedicated, delicate, and redundant work with my hands. Even with the physical pain it was life giving. My accessories brand, called Anamu, was a little side hustle launched with a party in my friend's backyard and sold on Etsy and at local craft markets in Los Angeles.

I did not start this company because I wasn't busy enough. Not feeling creative made me crazy enough to initiate more work as an outlet for creative expression. The sound and motions of the sewing machine were my meditation after a long day at work. Acupuncture ultimately relieved physical symptoms to let me do both jobs without pain. Despite having a creative outlet and a job that allowed me to make a difference in the world, I'd begun to wonder how I could work and exist differently in my day-to-day.

About two-and-a-half years after joining TOMS, instead of seeking to move within the company, it was time for me to leave. I loved the company, but start-up life was demanding, and I saw and experienced firsthand how the long hours and requirements can easily take over your life. I also saw the rewards that came of it, like exciting growth, impact, and recognition. But I knew that the pace and devotion necessary for the company to reach the next level did not match what I wanted from my career and life at that point. I wanted a straightforward 9 to 5 where I could be creative *and* have a shot at a more balanced personal life—and make more money. I gave my resignation at the same time that my boss delivered the news of a major pay raise. It was too late.

In my new role, I was marketing director for One Colorado, a boutique alfresco shopping center in Pasadena, California, close to where I grew up. I worked with the retail tenants, local organizations, and media to engage the community within an inspiring retail setting. I loved the location and thrived in my daily work. The property, with its central courtyard for gatherings and events, was a beautiful example of commerce-meeting-community.

My sister lived five minutes away and had just had her second child. This new life, with an easier workload and shorter work hours, allowed for lunch break visits and early dinners with her and my nieces. I even got to meet up with my then-boyfriend, now husband, Joe, for happy hour whenever we wanted. Sitting at a bar, enjoying his company with a cocktail in my hand by 5:20 p.m. felt like a brand-new world. I'd made the right choice.

One year into my sweet gig, Joe was presented with an

incredible job opportunity. He'd been working his way up the ladder in the energy industry with the goal of living and working internationally. The job was based in London, and he asked me to go with him. Saying YES changed the course of my life. But it wasn't an immediate yes.

As much as I planned to travel throughout my life, I never considered living anywhere other than Los Angeles. I *loved* LA. My entire personal and professional network was there—my family and friends. But I also knew that I loved Joe, and I was not ready for our relationship to end. My mom helped seal the deal when she said, "You love each other, and he wants to do this with you. Go have an adventure. You can always come back."

I knew she would feel that way. My parents had been on many adventures and are the poster children of resilience. At eighteen and nineteen, they left their native country of Colombia to live in Australia where they welcomed my sister and me into the world. When I was eighteen months old, we went back to Colombia for a few years before immigrating to the United States of America. In both cases, my mom and dad started with nearly nothing but faith and an excellent work ethic. If they could say *YES* to those adventures, full of unknowns, financial insecurities, and language barriers, I could certainly go on this one where we had financial security, spoke the same language, and didn't have to care for children.

In London, I discovered two surprising things: One, it can be really hard to make friends and build a new sense of community as an adult. Two, I enjoy being a homemaker. I relished in creating and maintaining our home while Joe worked.

I got to know London while making our flat a home. Needing

things like dinnerware and bedding meant going to unfamiliar stores. And going to stores meant exploring on the High Streets (what they call Main Streets in England). I got to know different neighborhoods by walking and shopping around the High Streets. I loved getting on the tube and buses and stepping out into a lane of new possibilities.

Big stores like the beloved UK department store John Lewis felt like a Target-Macy's-IKEA combo and provided a lot of the basics that we needed, quickly and easily. It was a relief to have John Lewis as a resource, but the independent shops on the smaller, tucked away High Streets made getting to know and live in London the pleasure it was.

By popping in and out of shops and talking to the Shopkeepers, I became acquainted with the local personality—the people, the materials local artists liked to work with, and the aesthetics of the neighborhood—through the objects on display. I saw everything in the stores as present-day cultural artifacts, full of information for me to glean. I was thankful for these stores and wondered what kind of experiences I would offer people in my own shop one day.

My visa allowed me to seek employment, but we did not know how long we'd be in London. Since Joe's job was project-based, we could have been there three months or three years. So, I decided to pursue interests that could become my employment, such as shopping at flea markets. The thrill of the hunt was a favorite past time in LA which launched my first official business, Anamu. I closed it before moving across the pond, but my love for exploring flea markets remained. Due to our temporary living arrangements and limited space, I couldn't justify buying and keeping every little thing that caught my eye. So, naturally, I set up an online store to sell my finds directly to people back in the States. I called it *The Pond Market*, and it served as a playing and learning ground for my Shopkeeper Dream.

I continued working on my personal blog, one that I started in LA while making my handbags and jewelry. The theme evolved into sharing my interests, novice graphic designs, and stories and photography from our adventures abroad. This led to a few contract jobs, such as taking photos for a blog's retail series and scouting emerging designers for a new marketplace—a Barcelona-based company that was, unfortunately, too far ahead of its time.

People seemed to enjoy what I shared, and some even entrusted their visions with me. I had so much fun creating the blog while teaching myself Adobe Photoshop and Illustrator, basic HTML, CSS coding, and the ins and outs of my DSLR Rebel T2i camera. I spent hours upon hours googling my way around these new worlds, the visual and graphic design realms that I lusted over while at TOMS.

I developed a love for design stores that I hadn't tapped into while I was living in Los Angeles. Design of all forms is intentionally celebrated in London, and I became obsessed with design-related retail and hospitality-based experiences. I was exposed to a new world of possibilities for fresh, contemporary, and classic design through everyday objects, architecture, and interiors. Before long, I was a modern design enthusiast, even if I couldn't fully express it in our tiny, temporary, and sparsely furnished flat.

Joe and I were newly engaged when we moved to Kuala Lumpur, Malaysia, for another one of his work opportunities. Living in KL and traveling around Southeast Asia reconnected us to nature while simultaneously throwing us into a world of gleaming mega malls, time-worn row house shops, and makeshift markets and street stalls. It was a sensory overload in a wonderful way, balanced by a lush tropical background everywhere we turned.

A new home-country led to a new way of creating. My Malaysian visa did not permit employment and The Pond Market didn't translate as well from our new geographic location. I considered pivoting what I sold to locally handmade goods instead of vintage and antique finds, but it didn't take long for a more intriguing idea to find me.

Aside from inexpensive yet well-made vintage pieces, I'd never worn nice jewelry, let alone actual gems. As a bride-to-be, I felt highly aware and protective of my diamond engagement ring and, not finding a product that would protect it from damage or loss while swimming and working out in the gym, I created Ring Cozy. Ring Cozy was an activewear accessory that I designed, manufactured, and sold online through my own e-commerce store. I created the prototypes on our dining room table using neoprene from mall-purchased iPad sleeves. Malaysia is a popular destination for divers who use neoprene suits, so it was shocking and annoying that I couldn't find a neoprene fabric supplier there. I eventually schlepped sixty pounds of neoprene that I purchased during our holiday in Australia back to KL to get a finished product.

Thanks to what I learned through my side hustle projects in Los Angeles and London, I designed the logo, website, many iterations of the packaging, and shot all the photography myself. Unlike my previous side-hustle projects, I believed that the Ring Cozy had big potential to scale and make a lot of money. I was encouraged by the feedback from my proof-of-concept audience, and it felt good to create a product that was entirely unique and useful to people with similar concerns about their beloved jewelry.

Unfortunately, Joe was not satisfied at work, and he decided to resign. This meant we'd be leaving a place where we had seen ourselves living for a long time—a place where we had started to build a small but solid group of friends. We imagined sharing the home we were living in with children of our own. Instead, we pivoted and imagined a new plan for the next chapter of our lives.

RALEIGH, THE PORT OF CALL

We returned to the States without a job relocation to guide us, and we were open to where our next home would be. Raleigh, North Carolina, was on our radar because Joe owned a condo in the heart of the city's downtown, and, at the time of our repatriation, Raleigh was at the top of every publication's list of best American cities to live in. When he purchased the condo years prior, he intended to keep it and live in it as a home base between jobs. That quickly changed when he accepted a new project in LA just weeks after closing on the condo. He packed his bags for the relocation and put his condo on the rental market. Two weeks later, at a wine bar in Pasadena, I approached him with my hand outstretched for a handshake and said, "Hi, I'm Ana Maria. I just wanted to say hi because I think you're cute." I never could have imagined that saying YES to a flirtatious urge would one day have me living and traveling the world with my partner in life and one-day calling North Carolina our home.

Moving to Raleigh was purely a lifestyle choice. We didn't know a single soul or have jobs waiting for us. What we did have was a mortgage that was less than the rent we'd pay in the other cities we'd considered. Raleigh also seemed to have the slower pace of life we were looking for at the time. We wanted a small yet vibrant urban existence, and we wanted to be near plentiful green spaces, lakes, mountains, and beaches. And a great airport was important because we wanted to continue to travel extensively and might need to travel for future jobs.

Our furnishings and personal belongings were in a storage unit in LA. It was time to pull them out and have movers truck them across the country to be used and enjoyed again. Joe and I decided to drive cross-country too. We hadn't owned a car in years, but knew we'd need and want one in Raleigh. We bought an old but reliable green Ford Escape from Craigslist and off we went, via Route 66, into a new adventure.

I was one month pregnant when we rolled into Raleigh. The pregnancy was literally and metaphorically symbolic of a new era. Joe was consulting for a company in California, and I was running Ring Cozy full time. I loved Ring Cozy, but I started to feel like an imposter as "the face" of the product since I wasn't a gym rat and fitness fanatic like 99 percent of the people who bought, used, and loved my product. I'd also lost the bandwidth for making them. I was sewing each one at home and getting Joe's help with the gluing stage and finishing touches as fast as I could sell them.

I spent a year and a half looking for manufacturers in the US and overseas, but no one wanted to take on my design's tiny details. When a manufacturer was up for the challenge, they couldn't get to the finish line. The effort to take production off our various dining room tables—from Kuala Lumpur to Los Angeles to Raleigh—was an incredibly frustrating one. I wanted to scale manufacturing so I could focus on sales and marketing, but I kept running into brick walls.

Meanwhile, I was pregnant with our first child, and all I wanted to do was nap and nest. Between production woes, feeling like I might not want to be Ms. Ring Cozy for the long haul, and realizing that my body and time were no longer my own, I reckoned that the cottage industry I'd started was ending. I'd been here before: another move, another home, another way of creating.

I was over the moon to shop locally for goods to make our modern condo feel cozy and special. I was tapping back into homemaking and connecting with small shops like I'd come to appreciate and love in London. Except this time, our home was fully ours to play with, no rental hacks needed.

Around this time, I was walking in our downtown Raleigh neighborhood when I saw a blanket in a shop window—just the right touch to warm up our new living room. I stepped inside, greeted the shopgirl, and immediately went to the blanket. As I moved my hands to pick it up, the shopgirl informed me that the blanket was part of the display. It turned out that my perfect blanket was from Target, and I was disappointed. I have nothing against Target, but if I wanted to buy a blanket from Target, I'd go to Target. I wanted to shop locally for our home, but the options were slim. Having already opened myself up to doing something beyond Ring Cozy—and a lifetime of dreaming up stores through school projects and visions every time I walked and drove by empty storefronts—I knew that I had arrived at the right time and place to realize my Shopkeeper Dream.

MY WHY

I always thought that if I opened a store, it would feature clothing and accessories. As a kid I'd spend hours drawing clothing designs with my colored pencils, and my collegiate studies in fashion merchandising supported that passion. But, while a love for personal style remained, my medium for self-expression had found a new home in design. No pun intended.

After furnishing my first apartment in downtown Los Angeles and living overseas with Joe in prefurnished spaces, I had developed a reverence for the at-home experience. No matter how permanent or temporary a home may be, from a fully furnished apartment to an extended hotel stay, there are always ways to make your space feel personal and special. From mementos you place on a shelf to everyday items like a fruit bowl that makes you happy when you look at it, home is where we can fully express and immerse ourselves in creativity to benefit our well-being.

I have a deep connection to the objects I choose to bring into my life and our home. Not in a materialistic sense, but from a place of appreciation deeply rooted in my upbringing.

I was four when my mom, sister, and I arrived in Los Angeles, California. My dad, who had immigrated from Colombia the year before, picked us up at LAX and just like that, we were reunited as a family, ready to start our new life in the US. Our apartment was a tiny, outdated two-bedroom unit in a quiet little city called South Pasadena, known for its excellent schools and safe neighborhoods. My dad had done a lot of research, planning, and executing. It was no accident that our new apartment was across the street from what would be our elementary school. Everything inside of our new home was as intentional as our address. Our Mickey and Minnie Mouse bedsheets welcomed us into American pop culture. The decorative pieces my dad placed around the house, sourced mostly from thrift shops and yard sales, showed us that he had intentionally created a home for us.

My dad was always looking to level up with the next best thing we could afford—from a new car lease and TV to a new-to-us home to hold it all. We moved a lot within the LA area, and despite the reasons and subsequent turmoil, my parents brought gratitude and intentionality to every interior reset. A decorative ceramic cactus here, a wooden decoy duck there. Whatever the object was, if it was brought into our home, it was purposefully placed with love and appreciation.

While my dad did most of the treasure-finding, my mom was the expert at bringing it all together. Guests would always comment on how good it felt to be in our home. It felt warm and inviting, just right with personal, unique, and interesting touches everywhere you looked. No matter how many times we moved and how many shuffles and arrangements the objects we lived with went through, my parents created a joyful experience for everyone who walked through our door to spend a little or long time with us.

I wanted to create a similar environment with my store through unique and lovingly displayed merchandise. I wanted to create the kind of shopping experience that I'd come to love in the small shops I encountered while living and traveling around the world, shopping experiences that were full of delight, discovery, and intention. I loved the modern-leaning design stores the most because there something had always been reimagined—an object made of surprising materials or techniques or one that just worked, looked, and felt better than previous versions thanks to craftsmanship and ingenuity.

A simple yet highly effective silicone doorstopper by *Droog* I purchased in a tiny shop in Clerkenwell, London, would set me on the design store path. When we were living in London, we needed a doorstopper to use in our flat. I was excited to discover a version of one that I'd never seen or considered until walking into that tightly curated small shop. A store dedicated to discovering practical design-led objects, like the doorstopper, did not exist in our newly adopted hometown.

The few stores that did exist landed more in the general gift shop category with modern design pieces mixed with slapstick greeting cards and novelty gifts. As for the local furniture market, there were a couple of independent retailers that leaned toward the mid-century aesthetic, and they featured few, if any, decor and functional objects. The rest of the independent offerings were firmly in vintage, antiques, Southern traditional, Southern eclectic, and the then-emerging modern farmhouse stylings.

Larger stores like West Elm and Crate & Barrel were nearby but didn't hit the mark for me as a shopper. They were heavy on the mid-century modern stylings at the time. I wanted to showcase contemporary objects and aesthetics of *today*, not yesterday or what has been. I wanted to celebrate the fact that the objects we live with can help us experience our everyday lives better.

Experience Your Everyday would become our store's motto and mantra. At the time, the "spend money on experiences, not things" concept dominated the social conversation, emphasizing spending money on dining or travel experiences. I found this viewpoint pointless because we *use things* to *do* things like dine and travel.

Because I wanted to help people enjoy their homes and everyday rituals through considered objects, I found myself on a mission to support my customers' well-being one coffee mug and table lamp at a time. I saw an exciting opportunity to elevate the home experience through highly intentional designs that were simple yet intriguing, and functional yet fun to use. By fun, I mean that they delighted users by looking and feeling good to use, not because an object had a silly cat face on it, though that can be fun too. I would offer a different shopping experience in our new hometown by sharing designs from around the world through a playful and contemporary lens.

The aesthetics of my product mix were clear in my mind, but when people asked what I'd carry, I'd reply, "Designs from around the world," and it seemed like visions of eclectic boho vibes a la Pier 1 or World Market danced in their heads. My vision for the store was MoMa Design Store meets Muji, a combination and description that more often than not led to blank stares from people who weren't familiar with either (insert flashback to my college e-commerce presentation here). My concept was unique for my market area, a fact I believed would work in my favor.

My store would be a port of sorts, a place for receiving and celebrating designs from afar that were previously unavailable and unknown in our region. We would also "export" local emerging designers who shared our ethos. The priority would be to establish the global and modern angle with "imports," and local "exports" would come after we got to know our community and our community got to know us. When I laid out my vision to my husband during an informal brainstorm for the name of the store, he confidently offered: Port of Raleigh. *Ding, ding, ding.* And so it was.

LAUNCHING THE STORE

It was rainy and windy, but in my mind, birds were singing, and butterflies were fluttering in the sunlight. I had just picked up the city-approved engineering plans for PofR's buildout and was riding a high. I walked home with thick, heavy rolls of blueprints tucked under my arm and a joyful skip in my step. Everything was coming together. I was a new mama and a new business owner ready to launch my Shopkeeper Dream.

Our daughter, Hazel, and the store were the same age on paper. PofR's business incorporation date was one day before she was born, and I received the final lease agreement via email on her date of birth. Months later, between endless construction, business to-dos, and diaper changes, the store was nearly ready to open for business.

I could not wait to hang my "OPEN" door sign. City inspectors, however, were perfectly fine to keep us in limbo. Sure, it's their job to be thorough, but I came to believe that they justify their job by demanding seemingly unnecessary changes at the business owners' expense. It seems as though something must be found to be off or wrong. That newly installed sprinkler in the middle of our 8x10 foot backroom? It needs to be moved just one inch closer to the door. The bathroom we just finished drywalling and installing based on the city-approved plans? Make it ADA compliant after all, even though, unlike restaurants, shops are not required to offer restrooms to the public.

The experience was frustrating to say the least. Since we needed the official sign-off from the city inspector before we could begin moving furniture and merchandise into the store, every "fix" delayed our move-in date. While our contractor and his subcontractors applied the final finishes to the space, a warehouse of stacked cardboard boxes full of merchandise grew in our one-bedroom condo. The timeline started to feel like a major holding pattern, and the boxes were a daily reminder.

Small Business Saturday was on the horizon, so I enthusiastically ordered #SmallBizSat goodies in anticipation of having opened our doors by that weekend. Even though PofR did not launch by that date, the celebration went on—a *pre*-celebration if you will. On Small Business Saturday morning, we were not yet cleared to occupy the space, much less for the public to enter, so I set up a small folding table by the door, covered it with the swag I had ordered, and prepared an email sign-up list for anyone who wanted to be notified of our opening date.

I invited the few locals we knew to come peek at the space — from outside, of course—and posted the event on Instagram, inviting our twenty or so followers with the promise of a free tote while supplies lasted. I thought that maybe, *just maybe*, enough people would stop by that we'd run out of all fifty bags. I even hand-stamped the PofR logo I'd designed inside each bag to make them commemorative (ha!).

It felt like a moment because I'd been a fan of Small Business Saturday since its launch about five years prior. The day is not about sales or gimmicks. It's about celebrating the little guys on the block, a counter to the big box stores' Black Friday. It's also a brilliant and generous American Express marketing campaign, and I'm not mad at it. Collectively, with a major marketing machine behind them, the little guys can feel pretty mighty. And I was finally joining "the little guys."

By any standard, my pre-celebration turnout was little. Within three hours, my Small Business Saturday event saw five people, three of whom walked away with a commemorative bag. It was a moonshot idea with hardly any lift since I didn't know many people in town and our store's block was extremely up and coming. But my spirit was not dampened. With our *Arriving Soon* signs covering the windows and an empty waiting-to-be-moved-into space behind me, my Shopkeeper Dream was unfolding right in front of me.

Opening day, or rather night, finally arrived, just in time to welcome Christmas shoppers. Everything inside the store glowed under the newly installed lights, seemingly radiating and pulsing along with my excited anticipation. And dread because nothing had price tags.

We were granted our Certificate of Occupancy (COO) two days prior and had moved the boxes out of our condo and into the store as quickly as possible. A few friends had kindly stopped by to help unpack boxes of merchandise, but for the most part, it was just Joe and me removing endless rounds of paper and cardboard while cleaning and touching up the remaining bits from construction and making final adjustments to installations. Hazel, not yet crawling, bounced in her Baby Bjorn lounger, or laid on the floor on a moving blanket. I was high on adrenaline, fueled by the determination to open our doors by 5 p.m. on First Friday, a night when we could attract more eyes and visitors since people would be out and about. Price tags be damned.

Our OPEN sign was the first indication to my customers that no detail of their experience was overlooked. I didn't want the generic blue-and-white sign I saw in every small business; I wanted every part of the Port Raleigh retail experience to be cohesive. I designed our sign myself because I couldn't find one that delivered the message and aesthetic I wanted for PofR. When I officially hung the open sign on the glass door and greeted our first guest with what I'm sure was the goofiest smile they've ever seen, I felt the power of that first impression, the one I carefully and painstakingly created after years of imagining what my store could be. It was surreal. So much energy from so many people had gone into making that moment possible. I was exhausted, elated, and relieved to finally be in *the* moment—opening day at my shop, my Shopkeeper Dream come true. And yes, we managed to sell products that night without price tags on them.

portofraleigh

Checked in this AM and found that there are now over 500 of you beautiful people following along in this retail journey – thank you!!! To think of all the steps taken to be here now is mind-blowing. Amazing what's possible with daily actions, endless support from friends and family, and a crazy sense of optimism for your passion and community. This shot is of the shop space being prepped for the concrete floor in October. Looks much different now, right? #tbt #stepbystep
JANUARY 7, 2016

Add a comment...

BURNING OUT
TWO YEARS LATER

I wanted to burn the place *down*. The most wonderful time of the year was just around the corner and, as I was decorating the store with tinsel and holly, I was fantasizing about leaving it all behind. My Shopkeeper Dream had secretly become a nightmare. I couldn't express it to anyone because I'd be complaining about the privilege of getting to work a dream that I had imagined since the fourth grade. A dream that I so purposefully and joyously brought to life.

My new Shopkeeper Dream was now my Shopkeeper Life, and for a time it had felt exhilarating, a natural fit. I was building something meaningful to me and, hopefully, valuable to others. I was having fun meeting new people and sharing items that I loved. Between merchandising the sales floor and posting content on Instagram, I was fulfilling my need to create daily. Joe and Hazel were in the store often, so I'd nurse her and play in between customers. My personal and family life were blending seamlessly into my new business owner one. Or so I thought.

In the early days of the business, I'd take a moment for myself in the back room before opening the store. I'd give thanks for my dream come true, for the people who would walk through the door, and set intentions for a successful day. I had great days fueled by the novelty of the entrepreneur high. But during the second year, as the store's operations became more routine, I stopped starting my days that way. The new routine became unlocking the door, placing my bag and coat in the back room, and immediately getting to work. There was no pause for reflection and gratitude—the work behind the work. I lost the energy for my purpose. Even when I was in good spirits, the appreciation for this special place and time faded into a brilliant burnout just as the store turned two years old.

Raleigh had experienced a glorious autumn, my favorite season, and I'd missed playing in its essence entirely. I knew that launching a store would be demanding on all levels, but living it, especially as a new mom, was more than I could have imagined. Hazel was now two and a half, and I'd begun to resent my fourteen- to sixteen-hour workdays. I had spent the year building and launching the online store, coordinating in-store events to engage with the community, working on days off to set up and break down art installations, and staying late to host related parties. These were all things that I wanted to do and enjoyed doing, but at the end of the day and no matter how much fun it all was, I was stretched thin. I needed help running the store and was slowly losing sight of what I was working for.

As December neared, the negative energy that permeated my bones and created chaos in my mind was something I'd never experienced before. I had worked hard and long in past jobs, but this role and business was all on me. Compared to my past businesses, my present stack of hats—business owner, operator, buyer, sales associate, janitor, online store manager and shipper, marketer, photographer, copywriter, event coordinator, and mom and wife—carried infinitely higher time, financial, and energetic investments. The internal landscape I found myself in felt new and scary to my nervous system and mental health. To make matters worse, I needed to focus, be merry, and get through the holiday season, our busiest time of year. I was a professional retailer running on fumes.

Throughout the first two years in business, I was consumed with guilt for not being with my daughter the way I wanted and believed that she needed me to be. My thoughts looped with *could've, would've, should've* scenarios around work and motherhood. Postpartum hormones affected me more seriously than I understood at the time. Hormonal changes and implications lingered, but I was too busy starting and growing a business while learning how to be a mom and a Shopkeeper. I often cried in the store's back room while looking at photos and videos my husband had texted to me. He had decided to be with Hazel full time while I worked on my dream.

One afternoon, the store was quiet, and Joe was a few blocks over with Hazel at an outdoor musical performance. He sent me a video that showed her from behind, standing alone and confident in her presence. She was paying close attention to the artist singing and playing guitar on the stage and slowly bent her knees, bobbing up and down, moving and feeling the music. She was having a beautiful experience that I wasn't a part of. I broke down. There I was, standing around waiting for customers to come into the store, watching the clock until I could close and be back with my daughter, who was just two blocks away, while I witnessed the moment from a screen.

Back-room crying sessions, emotional tug-of-wars, burnout... it all caught me by surprise. I've always loved digging into my work, so why was I not loving *this* work? This was my dream! Probably because I was postpartum and the weight of "doing it all" was heavier than anyone or anything could have prepared me to experience. When I started to get out from under the weight, I didn't even recognize the new version of me. I kept trying to apply my past work abilities, mindsets, and energies to the present and would beat myself up for not meeting my high expectations.

The past I kept comparing myself to was a point in my life when I had all of the time and energy in the world to devote to work and personal pursuits without affecting anyone else, including my supportive and patient partner. I could never have predicted the internal conflict and despair I would feel in juggling a new business and a new family all at once. And this was with Joe taking on most of the domestic and parental duties. I thought I was mentally stronger, wiser, and well-enough prepared to take on the challenges of motherhood and shopkeeping. Little did I know that my emotional and spiritual maturity were just barely coming into their own. And that postpartum hormones had hijacked my brain.

GETTING THE SPARK BACK

I was on an emotional roller-coaster ride. As roller coasters go, with every drop, there's a high point that follows. In the lead-up to wanting to burn the store down, PofR and I were featured in *Design Milk*, a respected and adored design industry blog. It was a major point of celebration for my family and tiny team, and for our customers who were readers and fans of the blog. Some even said that it was a proud and big moment for Raleigh. The feature made me feel like I was doing something right, despite my internal turmoil, and I am forever thankful to have caught the eye of a *Design Milk* editor who happened to live in Raleigh.

One of the questions in the interview was, *If you could give one piece of advice to someone who wants to follow a similar path to yours, what would it be?*

My answer:

"Understand that it's a lifestyle. Unless you're flush with cash and can hire a team of people to do everything for you, including being in the store with your customers, then you are it. At least while you're starting. I've worked office jobs and run my online-only stores. Operating a physical retail business is so different than doing something on your own, at your computer, on your own time. And you never fully clock out, so you better love what you're creating and sharing. Loving the community you're doing it in helps too!"

I loved what I was creating and sharing, and the community where it took place, but I did not love *how* I was doing it. In fact, I was trying to convince myself that my present way of existing was simply the cost of living the Shopkeeper Dream. Despite my somewhat cheery disposition in the full interview, and on a daily basis in-store, I was exhausted and ready to be supported. I finally had to stop and ask myself *If this is what I feel like inside, how is all of this showing up in my business?*

I was also tired of *would've, could've, should've* narratives. I was done saying and thinking things like, *I'm not doing enough to promote the online store*, and *I'm not taking enough photos for Instagram*, or *I'm not doing enough events for the community*, and *I'm not doing a good enough job at being a Shopkeeper*, or my favorite, *I'm not doing a good enough job at being Mom*.

While those statements may have felt true in the moment, these thoughts were counterproductive noise that left my head spinning into more madness. It was all madness because *I was already enough*. New considerations and choices needed to be made for what I wanted the store and my lifestyle to look and feel like. I started to recognize the need for slowing down and taking personal inventory.

As a new year began, I closed the store for a two-week winter break and headed to the mountains with my family. I needed time away and distance but, since both of my part-time employees would be on family vacations of their own, pressing pause on operations was the best solution. The store would be okay.

We had smashed our sales goal for the holiday season and, though I wanted to be open for customers enjoying their time off, I also knew that January was the perfect time for a rest because it was our slowest month.

Time away from the sales floor was spent snuggling with my family, playing in the snow, and staring at long-range views with a warm drink in hand. This period of slowness, reflection, and setting new intentions felt reinvigorating, and I was ready to have fun working in my Shopkeeper Dream again.

My husband and I kicked off the store's third year with fresh paint and a deep clean. More importantly, I fell back in love with my Shopkeeper Life. Refocused and motivated, I made plans for personal and operational changes to achieve the work-life balance I needed, or at the very least try for a smoother juggle.

Energy shifted in what felt like an instant. I went from *I should*, and *I have to*, to *I get to*. I felt lighter and more creatively fulfilled. I hired and trained additional help and found more time for myself and my family. It felt like the floodgates had opened and more people were finally taking notice of the store. Our sales reflected this free-flowing energy, as did the new stories I told myself. I released worries and trusted in the directions that my heart wanted to go, pairing this trust with the required operational nuts and bolts.

In addition to hiring new part-time employees, I set new personal boundaries, organized, and tidied up our books. I began writing monthly reports that helped save money on expenses and increase profits, all thanks to a consult from Chris Guillot of Merchant Method. We had our best year across the board: sales were up, the press were noticing us, our customer base and our Instagram reach grew, our team expanded, and we grew our purpose. I hadn't felt this good and in-tune with the store's purpose, and with *my* purpose, since the store opened. PofR's third year felt like an effortless joy—like magic.

I was in a better headspace and started feeling like the business owner I had set out to be. I was enjoying living my Shopkeeper Dream on the daily. With postpartum hormones, mom guilt, and start-up steppingstones out of the way, I felt like the best version of myself again.

Just in time to rediscover the next version of me as a mother of two.

We eagerly anticipated the arrival of our second daughter, Nicola, in the spring of PofR's fourth year in business. Customers enthusiastically watched my belly grow. They, too, were ready to meet a new member of the PofR family. With more motherhood and shopkeeping experience under my belt, and a solid team to lean on, I felt optimistic and excited for how work and life were evolving. My plan was that I would take a three-to-four-month maternity leave while my team held down the fort. I'd support them from home and pop in as needed.

The kink in the plan? I was at risk of losing two of my three beloved part-time employees. Trying not to stress out and think about hiring new people to overlap and take over in my absence, I gave myself a pep talk that it would all work out. And by working out I meant selfishly hoping that it would take many, many, *many* months for my two collegiate employees to land new and full-time gigs after they graduated.

It didn't take these brilliant women long at all. They each gave their notice one month before Nicola's arrival. The first would leave in April, when my daughter was due, and the other in early June. I could not fathom creating the time or energy to hire and train new people as I prepared to hand over the reins of the store and give birth to a human who would need me. The store was buzzing and hitting its stride, and it could not operate solely with my remaining part-timer who worked on weekends and cared for her own child on weekdays. I tried to surrender to the situation.

I scrambled and sent an SOS to friends who were in retail to see if they were available to work the store during the weekdays and busy weekends. Asking and paying for help worked. Friends came to the rescue. After all my worrying about the possibility of the store losing momentum in my absence, and with new faces, all was well. The ad-hoc team took care of business beautifully and the store carried on, even with reduced operating hours here and there.

I was able to squeeze two months out of the temporary arrangement before I was absolutely needed back at the store. A few days before I was set to put on my Shopkeeper hat again, a new challenge tested the foundation of the balance I was working to achieve. My family received a diagnosis for our eldest daughter, and the need for invasive surgery was a possibility, with results unknown. By all accounts, she was and is fine, but the diagnosis threw in a very heavy consideration for us: *What does this diagnosis, and doing or not doing surgery, mean for her now? For her future? Where do we go for a second opinion? If I had to be at the store every weekday because I didn't yet have the staff, how would we manage the potential six-month recovery, four of which she'd be in a cast from the* waist down? How would Joe take care of a baby and a four-year-old in recovery? Could I just shut down the store and be with my family?

I wanted to shut down the store and be with my family. For a second time, I found myself ready to walk away from it all, though this time was for a very different reason with high stakes.

Joe and I agreed that shutting down the store then or in the near future was not a viable option. Back on the sales floor all by myself, I did my best to put on a happy face. But I was not okay. I shared the joys of Nicola's birth with everyone who kindly asked and accepted their congratulations, while keeping our family's news private.

Again, I forced myself to find gratitude in giving the store my personal touch. It often worked to distract me and create moments of joy, but mostly I was crying in the back room, feeling upset and resentful. Adding to the stress, I closed the store for fifteen to thirty minutes several times a day to pump breast milk in the back room. This required a schedule, but most days, I couldn't stick to it due to customers continuously coming in or lingering once inside. Usually, having customers in the store was a great thing, but when my breasts screamed that it was time to go, I felt an urgent desperation to kick everyone *the fuuuck ooouuut*. This was no way to operate a store, or pump.

When I could take a moment, I would lock the shop door, put up a be *back at _o'clock* sign, and sit in the back room with my setup, trying to pump—keyword *try*, my boobs never provided much through this method. Meanwhile, I braced myself for the jolt and rattle of the shop door from people's attempt to open it. We moved to baby formula sooner than later, and thank god for the option.

As the store gained traction with daily visitors, I faced other high-pressure instances while working solo. I barely ate, or barely ate well, because I couldn't find a minute in between customers. When I did, my meals were hurried and rarely satisfying. Same goes for having to use the restroom like a racehorse.

Working as the sole sales associate of a retail store you own and manage is okay in the early days when you're still new and visitor counts are low. But it's not physically or mentally healthy to operate that way once you pass the *too busy to eat or pee* threshold. Slower days offered a more manageable pace, but I never lost the impulse to watch the time or wait for the next interruption. I fantasized about office life, with its controllable schedule, and missed working from home when I could carve out the space and time I wanted and needed. I also fantasized about not being at the store at all.

Going back to work so soon after giving birth felt like déjà vu. Just like two years prior, finding value in the workload for the brick-and-mortar and online stores was hard. I felt like I was in the second year of business all over again, internally shouting, *I don't want to be here!* And with new additions: *I don't want to be a salesperson,* and *I don't want to be an operator.* So what did I deeply want and need?

This didn't feel like burnout, but it did feel like an evolution in my Shopkeeper Journey. Nicola's birth and Hazel's diagnosis were major crossroads for me and my family, and it was time to ask bigger and better questions for moving forward. Yet again, time to find my energetic spark.

PART II
PREPPING THE SHOPKEEPER

TACKLING THE PROVERBIAL TOOLBOX

I had so much more agency over my experience than I was aware of or allowed myself to believe. I tried to control things and found myself frustrated with circumstances that I didn't have to feel frustrated about in the first place. In those moments, I was unaware of what I needed to thrive and the innate power that I held to make it so.

I had a passion for what I wanted to share and the store I would create. I saw the tools in my toolbox as perfectly polished from years of working in retail and marketing. I had every reason to believe that opening a store was what I was meant to do. But between the joys and messes of motherhood, and the sheer excitement of pursuing a lifelong dream, I was blinded to internal and external obstacles of living that very dream.

I assessed my toolbox and launched my dream store with a resume approach vs. a heartset one. The resume approach leads with past work experiences, perceived strengths, and tested skill sets as your guide: it's *quantitative*.

What is more challenging, but more important in many ways, is taking a heart-led, or heartset, approach to launching a new venture. That is, seeing and being brutally honest about what scares you, what lights you up or what drains the shit out of you. Then deeply consider the season of life you are in; be more *qualitative* in nature.

A heartset approach *references* your resume to understand what you truly desire out of your day-to-day life and how to live that life the best way you can—now and in the future, personally and professionally. If your heartset is sparked and shining bright, a positive mindset will follow, readily finding value in your work while creating value for others. With less propensity to get frustrated, complain, and over-control.

Creating value is the point of doing anything worthwhile. But as entrepreneurs, we sometimes set out to create and offer value without sharpening the best tools in our personal toolbox. Those tools are the knowledge of what truly makes us tick—the good and the painful, our deepest desires—and listening to our intuition. When we go into business and pour our heart and soul into it without understanding our heart and soul, we can end up working through our ego, the part of us that criticizes, judges, and likes to operate from a place of fear or scarcity. We can struggle to fit into the business we set out to share and grow, unknowingly sabotaging our best intentions. This was me to a T.

These distinctions are important because the way that you and your customers experience the store, and the way your business operates and succeeds, has everything to do with your personal energies and how you show up. A brick-and-mortar retail store is an intentional place for people to connect through space, time, and objects. It's where value and energy are exchanged through mutually beneficial transactions, and where we have the opportunity for micro-experiences at every touchpoint. And guess what? You're the ultimate touchpoint! For this reason, you must know what makes you tick, dim, and glow brightly. Pairing this knowledge with the why for your business and personal life creates a more useful and comprehensive toolbox. A toolbox that benefits and creates value for everyone involved.

Key Takeaways
→ The resume approach is quantitative. It leads with past work experiences, perceived strengths, and tested skill sets as your guide.
→ The heartset approach is qualitative. It references your resume to understand yourself—what scares you, lights you up, drains you, and the season of life you are in—and what you truly desire out of your day-to-day life.

Take Inventory
→ What's on your resume that can support your Shopkeeper Dream?
→ What's in your heart that can inform how you launch and operate your store?
→ What do you value, and what kind of value do you hope to create through your store?

TAKE PERSONAL INVENTORY

A retail store's merchandise inventory is in constant ebb and flow. This inventory requires frequent and thorough check-ins to keep many aspects of the business in alignment for optimal operation. Your personal inventory is also like this. Your *life* is like this.

You must check in with yourself, learn to tune into your energies, and be willing to dig through the darkest corner in your Personal Back Room to search for the thing(s) that may be throwing everything off. It's easy to present a neatly organized store (or self) that looks like it has its shit together. But the back room, the stockroom, the storage room, whatever you call it . . . that's where things get real, and a closer look is required. This is the space inside of us where we pull up our sleeves, take a big breath, and go deeper.

Why do we need to go so deep? Because as a Shopkeeper, there will be slow days and moments when you will feel like you're in a glass fish tank surrounded by the things you think are worth sharing with your community and the world. Just you in your fish tank, hoping that someone comes in and likes something enough to buy it so that you can pay rent, yourself, and your staff while continuing to share the things that bring you joy. Just you in your fish tank, wearing your creative heart on your sleeve for all to see and critique by way of your taste, décor, and the objects you select, even how the entire store looks at any given moment. It can feel vulnerable. And the more clarity you have about why you're in this fish tank, the better and more enjoyable the swim.

This vulnerability makes it easier to focus the journey outside ourselves when starting out. I unknowingly focused on the externalities of my business ideas, leading with my work resume full of prior retail experiences and skill sets. I used external data points and checklists to fuel my vision. What I didn't do as well, or perhaps at all because it's not as easy to do, is take a journey inward to determine how best to operate and enjoy my Shopkeeper Dream. I confused knowing my skill sets and mindset with knowing my heartset, the part of me that intimately understands my fears and desires, and my optimal conditions versus my kryptonite. I was confident but my self-worth was questionable. Letting your heartset take the lead will yield vastly more positive results. For you, your business, and your community.

Digging deep into our psyche and desires isn't typically how we begin the *start and operate a business* conversation. But as creative business coach Holly Howard suggests, it should be the first thing that we do. She once shared that her clients often state they need a marketing or financial plan for their new or growing business. Holly counters that what they *really* need, first and foremost, is a therapist.[i]

Therapy is a vulnerable place. And in entrepreneurship, you need to be prepared to be vulnerable. It takes a lot of courage to share yourself, your passions, your interests, and your skills, to inevitably share parts of you that are unknown to yourself. It takes courage to put your valuable time, money, and energy into all of it. At times, you will feel vulnerable because your store is an expression of you. This is why it's vital to take personal inventory and fill your toolbox with better tools. When you feel that vulnerability creep in, and you will, you can reassure yourself and be confident in what you're doing, why you're doing it, and how you're showing up.

> "Don't ask yourself what the world needs. Ask yourself what makes you come alive, and go do that, because what the world needs is people who have come alive."
>
> — Howard Washington Thurman

Being alive requires *knowing what makes you feel alive*.

The sooner you know this, the sooner you and your business will thrive. It all starts with curiosity about yourself.

At every stage of the entrepreneurial journey—before, during, and after—we must honor ourselves and our business by being curious about ourselves and our business. Everyone's personal inventory checklist (or rather, questions) will vary, but I have found the prompts below to be universal for reflection. When we can make choices based on meaningful reflection, we can be less reactionary in the moment, resulting in fewer reactionary decisions and creating more peace within ourselves and our business. From this vantage point, we can see the whole picture and respond to challenges in more productive ways as they arise.

These prompts are more than Q&As: they are reflections to inspire action.

What's my personality type?
For example: If spending a lot of time chatting with people energizes you, you may be an extrovert. On the other hand, if chatting drains your energy and you're exhausted at the end of a highly social activity or day, you may be an introvert. Neither are indicative of whether you are a social person or enjoy being social—it's about the degree of energy that social engagement gives or takes from you.

How do I like to work? How have I worked best in the past?
Do you like to work in groups and collaborative settings or solo in your own office? Do you prefer environments buzzing with activity or quiet, highly focused settings? Think back to times at work or with hobbies where you felt at ease, flowed with energy, and expanded your self-awareness. When did you feel the opposite? Do you find yourself constantly engaged with others, or do you prefer spending time alone in focused work?

What comes easily or naturally to me?
What skill or activity feels effortless to you? What do you make look easy or natural? Often, it's what you enjoy doing or don't think twice about doing. This could also be where you find a state of flow. What do people notice and comment about you the most? Think back to the nice, supportive, and perhaps even surprising things people have said to you or about you.

What doesn't come easily to you or feel natural?
What feels like a chore? What do you bitch about having to do? What do you criticize yourself for not doing well? What roles and tasks create the most friction for you?

What do I do (or not do) out of fear, shame, or judgement?
What do you do that most often leads to procrastination? What feels retractive instead of expansive? What do you find yourself questioning or criticizing in yourself, your situation, or what you see in other people?

What's my relationship with money?
How did you perceive money when you were a kid? Why? How do you experience money today? Making money? Having money? Spending and giving money? What good would making more money create in your world and in your community?

In what ways might I sabotage myself?
How do you receive opportunities that are presented to you? How do you view your time? Your mental capacity? Have these views and actions (or non-actions) resulted in you feeling disenchanted, regrettable, envious, and generally low about the results? How could these self-sabotaging experiences be turned around through different responses and/or actions?

What activities and thoughts make me feel expansive?
What makes your smile go big and your heart open wide with possibilities and purpose?

When do I feel the most flow? Joy?
What thoughts, activities, and experiences feel effortless and joyful at the same time? When you do you feel the most focused, creative, and playful with your work and in your personal life?

What drains the shit outta me?
What feels like the opposite of flow and joy? What activities and

interactions consistently leave you frustrated and exhausted afterwards? From certain types of conversations to particular types of computer-based or domestic work, activities and interactions could be social or work-related.

What do I see the world needing? What do I see my local community needing?
What gaps, needs, or opportunities in the world—at large and close to home—do you often think about? What solutions do you often feel called to consider and perhaps act on yourself?

The clarity gained from taking personal inventory opens the path to asking ourselves better questions. Better questions lead to more awareness and better discernment. The better our discernment, the better our questions and responses become. It's a beautiful, powerful, and fruitful cycle.

This cycle reinforces curiosity.

We find our energetic spark when we say YES to our curiosities.

YES = Your Energetic Spark™

The spark inside of us is meant to glow bright, but it needs our energy to make it crackle and pop. Sparked energy helps guide our intuition for the best next steps in our journey. This energy guides us in making big and small decisions, creating boundaries, and building systems that support us and our business. Saying YES is meant to fuel our spark—it's meant to feel good. If the spark for your business ever fades or completely burns out, then instead of beating yourself up, or giving up, get curious about what you're feeling and why. Take personal inventory, receive answers, and follow through with your best intentions.

There's one more question to ask yourself:

What season of life am I in?

This is perhaps the biggest thing to take stock of at any stage of your business. Because at the end of the day, the Shopkeeper Dream is an opportunity to both create what you want to see in the world and how you want to experience it.

Are you a student, new parent, or caregiver? In the prime of your career, or retired and in need of a sea change? How do you plan to work in your daily responsibilities and set expectations accordingly? And, most importantly, where do you see yourself in five years? Ten years? Recognizing and honoring whatever the season is for you—and identifying the most important and nonnegotiable aspects of it—will define your experience and over all well-being.

Whenever people would share their Shopkeeper Dream with me and sought my advice, I was reminded of the romanticism around setting up shop to share something you love. One woman in particular was interested in starting a store in our neighborhood. She had already scouted locations, contacted potential vendors, and drafted a business logo. Now she wanted to hear what it was like to own and operate an independent store.

We discussed her vision for a children's boutique, resources, and her lifestyle. Her concept was beautiful, intentional, and stood a good chance of being well-received in our city. The resources were there: her daughter was older, so time and energy were available, a loan was secured, and her husband worked full-time, giving them the ability to take on the financial investment and risk. However, her family's lifestyle was the biggest challenge. They were a military family and could be given orders to move at any moment. They wanted to keep traveling, including an annual weeks-long trip overseas. More importantly, she didn't want to be at the store all the time.

I was excited for her Shopkeeper Dream, but I was also honest in sharing the commitment required to pursue that dream. Unless she planned to open with an employee from day one or to limit operating days and hours to suit her family's needs, she would be there all the time. It could take months or years to gather the resources to pay for support, depending on a range of practical and personal factors: profit margins, location, overhead costs, selling online, personal boundaries, skill sets, etc. I relayed that a store has the potential to become your lifestyle, which was a good or not-so-good thing depending on your personal inventory results.

Understanding this and weighing the options and reality of her current and desired future lifestyle, she ultimately decided not to move forward with opening her store and considered other ways to share her gifts and passions. She took excellent inventory of where she was in that moment, where she wanted to be in the coming years, and how to synch the two. Owning and operating a store didn't fit her lifestyle goals, no matter how much she fantasized about setting up shop.

I, on the other hand, had tunnel vision for my retail endeavor. I'd spent years walking and driving past empty storefronts, imagining what I could create inside of them. A long-held *one day* dream became a glaring *today* opportunity, and it felt like something that I had to do. Being in a new city and state, and being a first-time mama, were just details to fold into the equation. I took my daughter's birth occurring on the same day I received our lease agreement in my email as a sign that I was ready for the unknown of the two new worlds of Motherhood and Shopkeeping. I seized the moment in that season of my life and followed the energetic sparks in my heart to say YES, blinders on and all.

You may or may not feel like it's the perfect time, and you may or may not have a background in retail. All you know is that you have a desire to make your visions of the shop you want to create a reality. Regardless of your life season, you have a passion for what you want to do and how you want to share it in the world.

Do you jump in and accept the Shopkeeper Dream in the season you're in? Do you let the romance sweep you off your feet? Do you accept that by opening your store, you also open yourself up to major personal growth throughout the countless ups and downs?

Whether you're an immediate YES or are still considering the possibilities, perhaps the next example will help make the case for taking personal inventory early and often in your journey. If you're a current Shopkeeper, it's never too late to start.

Key Takeaways

→ Like a store's inventory, taking personal inventory requires frequent and thorough check-ins to align yourself for optimal operation.

→ Be willing to dig through the darkest corner in your Personal Back room to search for the thing(s) that may be throwing everything off.

→ Be prepared to be vulnerable. Your store is an expression of you, and it takes courage to launch your dream and put yourself out there.

→ The sooner you identify what makes you *feel alive*, the sooner you and your business will thrive. It all starts with curiosity about yourself.

→ YES = Your Energetic Spark™: You find your energetic spark when you say YES to your curiosities.

MAKE MONEY YOUR BEST FRIEND

The desire to make money is necessary to be successful in business. And yet, it was more complicated for me. Scarcity and self-worth around money is precisely what kept me energetically stuck. And I had no idea.

In the store's final months, I became aware of a personal block around managing, spending, and receiving money. It was 2020, a year that forced many of us to go within and ask a lot of questions. It was certainly a time of deep personal inventory-taking for me. I realized that while I loved pursuing my Shopkeeper Dream, financial wealth, to me, was very tied up with its success.

My personal worth had become about how much money I *wasn't* making with the store, even though in some ways, I was choosing to not make it through my modes of operation. Because my ego was so focused on making money, I felt insecure about it not coming in the way I'd hoped and needed to prove my success to myself.

I didn't always feel this way. In college, having learned from my parents' hard lessons in finances, I vowed that I would be a responsible high-earner, spender, investor, and saver. I observed my parents working in jobs that were physically laborious and really hard at times. Then, I watched them make some really bad choices on how to spend that hard-earned money. I now recognize that what I perceived as *bad* or *wrong* was simply part of their life's course in learning personal lessons while showing my sister and me how to launch differently in our own lives. Yet, these imprints gave me the deep desire, or dare I say *need*, to provide for myself financially through work that I felt called to do, not *had* to do.

I was eager to learn how to responsibly manage money, even more so after a school assignment had us reading and learning from *The Automatic Millionaire* by David Bach. The book's message about setting the intention to save and invest, and making the subsequent actions automatic, gave me a newfound commitment and road map to my financial goals. These goals and habits gained more traction when I started earning a salary. I took pleasure in what I earned and, for the most part, made good spending, saving, and investment decisions (according to me).

When I joined Joe in London, my salary and paychecks stopped, as did my automatic millionaire practices. With his job, he was able to provide for the both of us and I didn't have to work. At first, it felt like a foreign and uncomfortable concept, but I was open to what that could look like for me and for us. I remember when he gave me a card linked to our first shared bank account. I half-jokingly asked him, "How does this work? Do I run it by you when I want to buy a sweater?" His response was, "No, it's your money too. It's our money." I wanted to contribute to our new household, but not through traditional employment, or even financially. I was fully aware of this newfound privilege, so I chose to make the most of it and explored other paths. I created work for myself through freelance gigs and personal projects, and surprisingly found value in contributing to our household by caring for it full time. I finally learned how to cook!

Joe never made me feel like I needed to pull my own weight with finances. He enjoyed seeing me fulfill new and old professional and personal desires. I dove into the creative freedom that came with this time, space, and support and did my best to never take it for granted. Over the years, having one primary breadwinner in the household became our norm. My gratitude painted a new picture for our way of life. A way of life that my college-age self would have never imagined, and in some ways my Shopkeeper-self had never fully processed.

As life happened and choices were made, I lost touch with the flow of making, saving, and investing money on my own. In losing this connection, and not considering its loss before opening my dream business, I tormented myself as a Shopkeeper. I knew I wanted to build a thriving business as an entrepreneur, and I wanted to make money. I didn't understand why it felt so hard to believe that I could accomplish both. I'd throw trust and creativity to the wayside, subconsciously preferring to cruise with Ms. Fear and Mr. Scarcity controlling the wheel. Creating and enabling money stressors not only hijacked my personal well-being over time, but it also blocked the potential for the truest and best intentions I had for myself and my business.

Luckily, every time I caught myself, recognized my fears, and shifted my mindset to finding fun and love in the process, purpose, money, and opportunities flowed in—the proof was in the pudding. This was never clearer than in our third magical year, when I got clear on what I did and did not want, led with gratitude, and opened myself up to great possibilities. In closing the store, instead of wallowing in thoughts of failure because I didn't get to sell the store and turn a profit—ahem, prove success—I happily wrapped everything up with zero debt and some pocket change. In the end, my cause-and-effect experiences were never about money: they were about my heartset leading my mindset. When I trusted that my best friend called Money would be there, everything felt and operated better. Including myself.

So what was your answer to the inventory checklist question, **What's my relationship with money?**

If your response is anything less than, *She's my homie and I trust her endlessly*, then you might need to dig deeper. There may be opportunities to get clearer, build more trust, and to set up the tangible support systems you and your business need to thrive. You trust your best friends. You have fun with them. You don't worry that they're not going to be there for you—of course, they will be! Money and your business can work like this too.

Key Takeaway
→ Unknown personal blocks can hinder the potential for your truest and best intentions for yourself and your business.

Take Personal Inventory
→ What are your store's financial needs and expectations in your current season of life?
→ How can you let your heartset take the lead so that a healthy money mindset can follow?
→ How can you take the stress off of finances to find the fun and love in the process and purpose of your Shopkeeper Dream?

PLAN TO PAY YOURSELF ASAP

PofR was growing across the board, yet I was unaware that my drive to make a living off my passion was handicapped from reaching its full potential. Behind the scenes, my relationship with money was manifesting in self-sabotaging ways. Frustrated with QuickBooks, after a second round of duplicate transactions in two accounts, I had thrown my hands up and couldn't be bothered to deal with it until tax time came around, as it does every year. My books were a mess, and I couldn't imagine prioritizing the funds to hire a bookkeeper for daily help. I figured I was okay as long as I knew what money was coming in and going out. The bank balance was all I needed, I told myself.

For the most part, that was true. But believing that kept me from operating in a way that could have helped our bottom line, and my mental state, expand for the better. I never did open-to-buy reports and the sort, and I didn't keep up with the reports that I had started in our third year to diligently review sales and profit margins every month. The heaviest subconscious weight was that I hadn't made a solid plan to pay myself.

I didn't pay myself a single cent in five years. I kept waiting until we finished paying off our $125,000 loan at the end of our fifth year—a monthly expense nearly equal to our rent—and for sales to be over $250,000. Only then would there be room to cut a check for the Shopkeeper. The business hit both of my self-imposed requirements, but their timing ultimately didn't matter. The devaluation had been done. I didn't value myself enough to pay myself. Every penny went back into the business. Responsible in a sense but, without a strategic plan to financially support myself and my family, I was betting on too many unknowns when there could have been so much more within my reach.

I was in a fortunate position to not have to take wages from the business to support myself and my family. And out of some combination of guilt and shame around living that privilege, I devalued myself for it. I fell prey to the martyrdom of entrepreneurship, noting that most people who start a business don't expect to take a salary or profits for the first couple of years. I understood that PofR, like many businesses, had a stretched-out path to profitability. Most of my retail peers had partners who worked full-time or were supporting themselves and their families through loans, savings, and investments. Some simply started out small with low-investment, high-return shops and grew organically to their fuller and bigger versions. Yet I took martyrdom too far.

We reached a quarter of a million dollars in gross sales toward the end of the fourth year. I finally considered adding myself to the payroll, but by that point it was too late. I was focused on getting our ducks in a row to sell the business. Taking a salary now would remove cash, and I wanted the books to be as cash positive as possible. I even reached out to a bookkeeper.

I wondered if the reason I hadn't made concrete plans to earn a salary was because I wasn't hungry enough. *What if I had needed my business to provide for my family, to put a roof over our heads and food on the table?* I took a guilt trip driven by a hypothetical threat that, at that point, was clearly not likely to happen. The reality is that the safety net—established through a lot of hard work and smart moves by my husband and our diligent savings and investments over the years—allowed me to take on the kind of risk that let me fall prey to the martyrdom of entrepreneurship. This hypothetical guilt trip undermined all the work, love, time, and energy I put into the business. It undermined and undervalued me, the Shopkeeper. Receiving compensation for work should be a given, regardless of your safety net.

I'll never forget a woman who walked around from shelf to shelf seemingly bewildered as to how a store like mine could ever make money. She was unfiltered and asked, "It's gotta be *sooo hard*, are you making *any* money?" Thank goodness I was having a good day, or I don't know what she would have done to my spirit. She was right. It was hard. And no; *I* wasn't making any money. The store was. We had positive cash flow and sales were growing double digits year over year. We just didn't have free cash flow yet—the kind of cash flow needed to responsibly pay myself (or so I told myself).

Not paying myself ultimately made me feel like the store was a hobby instead of a business, igniting A LOT of internal turmoil and self-doubt. I'd hear myself say things like, *All this work for what? What do I have to show for it?* If I wanted to spend that much time and energy on a hobby, I'd be a master potter or basket weaver. With all that I had, I wanted PofR to work, and I wanted it to work as a business. A business that justified the time I spent away from my family. A business that justified my husband taking time off from his career to support mine and be the full-time parent. If I wasn't bringing home the dough, then *what was I even doing*? I didn't expect to become a millionaire, but it would have been nice to cover our mortgage and then some. I don't want to define my self-worth by how much money I make, or don't, but paying myself for a business I built and nurtured should have been nonnegotiable. Establishing and sticking to a strategic plan for compensating myself monetarily as the store grew would have helped me believe more in the store's financial viability and in myself as an entrepreneur.

Your Shopkeeper Dream may stem from a personal passion, but chances are that you, too, want to make a living out of it. How will you make a living as a Shopkeeper? Plan for it by taking personal inventory to uncover and work through any blocks—money or otherwise—that could sabotage your biggest and most beautiful intentions for your retail dream.

Key Takeaways

→ Most entrepreneurs don't expect to take a salary or profits in the early years of their business. If this is your case, know you don't have to be a martyr.

→ Compensation for your work should be a given. Don't undermine or undervalue yourself.

Take Inventory

→ What does a strategic plan to pay yourself look like?

→ If your Shopkeeper Dream must provide a salary from the get-go, what are your monthly nonnegotiables for the store's and your personal needs?

→ If you're not getting paid (yet), then how do you answer the question, *What am I even doing this for?* How can you find value and excitement in what's been accomplished and the value you've created for others up to this point? How can this be expanded on your way to profitability?

ANTICIPATE YOUR COMMERCIAL + COMMUNITY ECOSYSTEM

When you open a store, you jump into the existing ecosystem that is your city and neighborhood, and put your faith in its potential, sustainability, and growth. Your store is part of a commercial + community ecosystem made up of landlords, business owners, local organizations, customers, service providers, collaborators, residents, and visitors alike. And just like other ecosystems, naturally occurring or human-made, thriving versus simply surviving depends on many factors.

During my time as the marketing director for One Colorado, the alfresco commercial property I worked for in Pasadena, California, I moved into a new role in the commercial + community ecosystem. I grew up visiting the shopping district that One Colorado is a part of and made many fond memories there as a teenager dancing in the courtyard to swing bands during summer nights and getting burgers at Johnny Rockets with friends. But working in it and for it gave me a new perspective on the dynamics at play.

Old Pasadena is a mix of corporate and independent restaurants, bars, cafes, retail stores, and service providers all within an easily walkable and discoverable cluster of several city blocks. You'll find hair and nail salons, art centers, fitness studios, and a cinema. All the merchants play off of each other. Pedestrian-friendly parking is plentiful, green parks buffer the perimeter, and residential and commercial buildings are mixed in, guaranteeing both daytime and after-work visitors. Old Pasadena is generally perceived as a safe and pleasant place to shop, dine, gather, work, and live because it is that place.

Retail districts work best when there are mutually beneficial energy exchanges in close proximity. When I selected my location for PofR, I had Old Pasadena as an example of the potential for Downtown Raleigh. I thought that I could jump into the ecosystem while being on the fringe of the district map. I was optimistic, and for good reason; when I opened the store Raleigh was on a massive upward trajectory. People were moving from major cities and downtown anticipated significant growth. There were sizable commercial, office, and residential investments with developments in progress.

I believed that my store would get in early, have time to establish itself, and, within a few years, reap the benefits of a booming downtown backdrop. I saw the potential for Downtown Raleigh to look and feel the way Old Pasadena did, and I believed that my store had a chance to thrive because of it. This didn't play out as hoped.

I learned that, like most city downtown areas, from a revitalization and financial standpoint, bars and restaurants get first considerations from landlords. This can make it hard for small retailers to open on highly desired main streets since bars and restaurants can more readily pay higher rent. Our downtown's main street remained primarily bars, banks, law and health provider offices, and restaurants that mostly operate as bars, not exactly a dynamic mix for the community at large but a work in progress, nevertheless.

It takes a village of Shopkeepers to make a thriving commercial + community ecosystem and, for the benefit of everyone, stores ideally share the same street or exist within a tight and walkable shopping district. We did not have a proper shopping district in our downtown. PofR was part of a sparsely dispersed collective of independent retailers with a shared desire to make it feel like we were all on Main Street together. We'd often refer customers to each other through writing recommendations on sticky notes, printer paper, promotional postcards lying around, or whatever unhelpful map people walked in with. It was time to create something more useful.

A handful of retail peers and I wanted to make it easy for locals and visitors to discover, walk to, and shop with all of us. We wanted to make it easy for people to play in our commercial + community ecosystem. During my third year of business, I cofounded DTR Independent Shops. The founding Shopkeepers pooled our collective resources and hired a local graphic designer to create a brand, website, and most importantly, a printed map and walking guide. The printed walking guide was key because, while most of our stores were within a doable walking distance, too often the shopper mentality was *out of sight out of mind*, or rather, *out of sight undiscoverable*. A few times a year, on those magical just-right spring and autumn days, people were more likely to walk more than a few blocks to the next shop. But for the most part, *the next shop* would be relegated to another day, or never visited at all.

The map only featured the independent shops. Not the restaurants. Not the bars. Just the merchants of curated goods that added their unique expression to the fabric of the community. Every single independent retailer in the downtown districts was included in the map, regardless of whether they were members of the DTR Independent Shops Group. It was not a pay-to-play map. A piecemeal approach would be a disservice to the end users and the businesses the map aimed to serve. Shopkeepers who did choose to join the retail collective, meaning they put money into establishing the group, were highlighted on the back side of the map and website with a full-color store photo of their choice, store name, location, and brief description. But everyone got to be in the game.

We were fortunate to have the support of our local downtown business alliance. Thanks to the efforts of a few Shopkeepers, the organization sponsored the printing of the maps and offered to support us as much as they could. They were happy to offer sponsorship because, at the time, their hands were tied when it came to launching promotions for only the small independent retail stores in the designated district. I learned a lesson in local-level politics: bigger-name stores (like a national pharmacy) as well as any small businesses with an added retail component (like a yoga studio selling branded T-shirts and towels) may dislike exclusion from any retail promotions.

The printed maps were beautiful and useful. They were proudly displayed in participating stores. The celebratory design and thoughtful weight and feel of the paper drew shoppers. The collective and tangible maps brought our dispersed village of Shopkeepers closer together.

One of the best reactions I personally experienced with the maps was with a gentleman who popped into the store to ask where he might find North Carolina magnets. We didn't sell any so I picked up a brand spanking new *DTR Independent Shops* map to show him where he could find one, then folded it back up and placed it in his hands. At that moment he said, "Wow, this is so nice, it's a souvenir on its own!" My heart smiled. That's why we created it, to collectively make our visitors' experiences, and our stores' visibility, better.

I loved being in the local business owners' club for the shared recognition. In that club—with food and beverage, services, *and* retail—there was a mutual appreciation for individual businesses and daily efforts. Beyond referring people to one another, we often engaged via transactions. For example, a coffee shop would buy decor from our store, and we'd hire them to cater an event. We were all living our dream, doing our part to contribute positively to the ecosystem we eagerly joined.

There's much to consider and tend to inside of your store, but it doesn't operate alone on a barren island. When you look beyond your window view and step into the commercial + community ecosystem, you can find ways to connect, engage, and thrive, even when the external conditions aren't ideal.

Key Takeaway
→ Your store is part of a living ecosystem you put your faith into. Surviving or thriving will depend on many external factors.

Take Personal Inventory
→ How will you engage with the diverse players in your ecosystem? From need-to to want-to? How might your expectations or boundaries of those players evolve?
→ How might you support your community members or work together for shared goals?
→ In what ways could your store actively participate in the ecosystem you'd like to thrive in?

OWN YOUR SHOPKEEPER TITLE

The most important player in a Shopkeeper Dream is the Shopkeeper. And to thrive within the commercial + community ecosystem you and your store will inhabit, the Shopkeeper must learn how to thrive within themself.

Part of thriving is owning and celebrating what you do.

Yet while I use the word and title of Shopkeeper in this book, and celebrate it, I rarely used it for myself during PofR's lifespan. "Shopkeeper," while clearly defining the role, always felt a bit outdated to me.

I identified as the store's "Owner," and in rare cases, "Founder." However, Owner and Founder never felt holistic. An owner can be someone who holds ownership in the business but has little to do with the daily operations, or someone involved in the operations but removed from the sales floor, working on the business versus working in the business. I wanted to operate like the latter, but my reality felt more like 90 percent IN the business and 10 percent ON it—a concept from the book *The E-Myth* by Michael Gerber and a message that would have been useful to reread many times over after opening the store. Like I said earlier, I was a salesperson, a janitor, an accountant (kinda), a buyer, merchandiser, shipper, office supplies manager, human resources manager, marketer, social media coordinator, photographer, website and e-commerce administrator, customer service representative—the list goes on. Calling myself Owner in written bios, conversation, and on my business card wasn't entirely accurate. I was *so much more*.

Founder seemed even less accurate. I hadn't started the store and brought on new leadership or sold to a new owner. Nor had I founded the store and was involved in ambiguous or singular ways. I was highly involved in very specific ways. I *was* the store. If I used the term Founder, it was followed by Owner for clarification.

It's a shame that I didn't embrace, celebrate, and use the title Shopkeeper because its basic definition is the owner and manager of a store! I was always proud of that, even if I didn't want to be the manager sometimes. I owned my shop; I managed my shop. All the hats worn were part of the Shopkeeper role. And managing the many hats required and resulted in different types of energies. Energies that I would later come to recognize as both superpowers and pitfalls.

Taking your personal inventory often and honestly will help you spot your own superpowers and opportunities to get back up again better, faster, and stronger after every pitfall. Making your dream come true is an empowering exercise, even when it feels impossible. So empower yourself by honoring and celebrating your Shopkeeper role and title in every moment you can.

Key Takeaway
→ A Shopkeeper is a person who owns and operates a small store. Yes, that's you.

Take Personal Inventory
→ What does each title — Founder, Owner, Shopkeeper — make you feel when you read, think, and say it? What connotations do each word bring up for you?
→ How might calling yourself a Shopkeeper affect your experience of owning and operating your store?
→ If your goal is to perform more as an Owner or Founder, what steps can you take now, as a Shopkeeper, to get there?

WARNING: Imposter Syndrome

You may or may not feel this, but if and when you do, know this: The way you share things and why you share them is nothing but authentic. It all comes from you. You can't fake your passion. If you try, you know it, and so does everyone else.

You may feel like you don't know some things (like how to run a store), but you do know what you want to share and why. THAT is and will be a major reason for your success.

PART III
PREPPING THE STORE

CHOOSE YOUR LOCATION

I'd heard it countless times: location, location, location!

Sure, I understood that to consider a location was to consider *everything*—available parking, foot traffic, neighboring businesses—but I fell in love with one location. My future storefront was a raw, empty shell in a newly constructed building ready to be transformed. Did it have parking? Yes, an entire parking deck attached behind the building and some street parking. Foot traffic? Not really, but it was next to one of the top restaurants in the city where locals and tourists flocked. If the restaurant could make a destination out of this corner, so could I. It also had residential apartments upstairs. What about neighboring retail businesses? Nope. Mine would be the first on my side of the building surrounded by a two-block radius of government buildings, parking lots, and vacant properties. *But*—the almighty *but*—the landlord told me about plans for the building's corner anchor, a new restaurant concept from their successful local restaurant group that was sure to revitalize this pocket of downtown. The best part of all was that this retail location was two blocks from our condo, perfect for our one-car family. With little available inventory to choose from, an urgent desire to open ASAP, and an exciting sense of possibilities—I took it.

I eventually made the store a regional destination. Unfortunately, my love for the interior of the location could not overcome the exterior challenges. Sure, we had parking, but most people preferred to park on city streets for their visit and not in our plentiful multi-storied adjacent lot. They'd drive around in circles, searching for a spot, or bail on a visit altogether. We did have retail neighbors, but it took several years. And that anchor restaurant I was told about when signing the lease? The one that was going to bring people to the block (because good food brings people to any block)? It never happened. Not only did it never come to fruition, but the landlord kept insisting it would. As of writing this book, eight years after I signed the store's lease, the supposed restaurant space still sits empty but for rubble on the ground, fallen and forgotten ladders, dirty windows, and tree-size weeds growing inside. It is such a sad sight. Not just for the building's retail tenants, but for the entire block. The residents who live upstairs and anyone passing by day after day only sees an unoccupied space that adds zero value to the streetscape.

In selecting my location, I did the best I could with the market data available at the time, but there's no denying that my starry eyes for the city blinded me. I imagine that a longtime resident might have seen my dot on the map through a different lens, a lens with more experience that knew the local culture, and perhaps even the landlord, more intimately. While I have no regrets about my choice, I can now stress the importance of a calculated approach to considering *everything* about a location.

I witnessed other entrepreneurs' thorough calculations in

action after PofR opened, but one example in particular stands out. A woman was doing research for opening a European gelato and coffee house. She loved my store, loved the restaurant next door, and wanted to be our neighbor. However, the franchiser had specific foot traffic thresholds they required their franchisee's locations to meet. After a few weeks of foot traffic studies, as well as likely reviewing more metrics I'm not aware of, it was determined that our block was, in fact, not the best location for her to set up shop. I was disappointed because in my mind, coffee and gelato were exactly what our block needed. It was what my store needed to help boost foot traffic to the block and encourage more frequent visits. She signed a lease several blocks away and is doing splendidly.

Setting up shop next to a beloved bakery or coffee shop can be gold for your business as it creates infinitely more opportunities to capture eyeballs and in-store visits. People eat and drink way more than they shop for curated nonedible goods, and when it comes to coffee shops, people are more likely to be in a lingering mood. I've seen Shopkeepers incorporate coffee and food into their store brand and physical spaces to create a true third place for their community and higher engagement for their business. It's a thing of beauty when entrepreneurs find their balance with a retail store and cafe all in one. When done well, it makes you wonder why either are ever done separately.

Sadly, I haven't seen or experienced the engaged *lingering crowd* play out as well with restaurants. Lunch and dinner crowds are, more often than not, singularly focused on their dining experience and allot time in their schedules just for that. If you're next to a restaurant, your best bets for capturing their visitors' attention are long waits to be seated and people enjoying a stroll after brunch. Both are nice, but neither are as great as the coffee-sipping crowd. People waiting to be seated for a dining experience are killing time in your store. Very few of these visitors will make a purchase or come back. The post-brunch crowd is usually catching up with friends and family, and they use the store visit as an opportunity to keep chatting while walking their meal off. Very few of these visitors make a purchase or come back. Trust me, you want the coffee crowd.

Beyond coffee shops, consider what a retail location means to you and how you'll marry that vision with what businesses and complimentary neighbors currently exist, or what shops are missing. For example, it's brilliant for a children's bookstore to be one block from a children's museum that makes it easy for families and caregivers to extend their outing without making another trip. Also brilliant, assuming a post-pandemic return to office life, is a gift shop on a block sandwiched by office buildings full of daytime workers who can run in at lunchtime or after work to grab a gift or something they need for their home. Low effort, high convenience.

My story of creating a stand-alone destination retail store isn't to say that a stand-alone location can't or won't work; it can and they do work: but there's often more in play than the physical address and four walls of the store, such as a specialty clientele like knitters or musicians. I chose to step into my would-be store with that house-hunting feeling of *this is home*. But it wasn't my home. It was a business, even if it was a very personal one. I got so caught up in the neighborhood I had picked that I favored a worthy challenge over the time-tested fundamentals of location, location, location!

Key Takeaways
→ Your storefront is a business. It's not your home, though it may sometimes feel like it.
→ A calculated approach to adjacent parking, foot traffic, and neighboring businesses will support your business tenfold.

Take Inventory
→ What is your heart's desire for your retail space? What kind of experience do you want to create inside of it?
→ What non-negotiables support your vision from a practical standpoint, such as price, square footage, and move-in readiness? What nonnegotiables would support your daily well-being, such as natural light or proximity to your home?
→ What can you find out about the landlord, the history of the building, and past tenants (if applicable) before signing a lease?

BUILD OUT THE DREAM

The ground was still gravel, plumbing was up for completion, lighting was to be specified, HVAC had to be installed, and the dividing wall for the adjacent space was yet to be erected. I had selected an extensive, expensive, and frustrating route.

I was the first tenant of this empty shell... a true blank canvas. The possibilities were initially very exciting; we could build anything inside of it! But as the costs of the basics added up, my list of sleek modular displays, statement light fixtures, and nice to have but not necessary floor trims and baseboards went out the window. What did stay was my vision of a yellow "shipping container" as the backdrop and back room (get it, Port of Raleigh?). This bold build-out would become our visual calling card.

As tenants, it was up to us to take on the buildout; we'd design and finish the space to our specs as approved by the landlord and the city. The landlord provided a Tenant Improvement Allowance (TIA), as is standard with most leases, that was intended to cover necessary work and permanent elements, such as walls, flooring, and HVAC. We'd pay the rest out of pocket.

When I signed the lease, I took the TIA amount (determined by the landlord's independently obtained market rate quotes from contractors) in good faith. But I should have worked with a broker and gotten independent quotes for permanent elements and negotiated the TIA based on said quotes. We had no negotiating power when the landlord's quote and the TIA proved to be extremely low. My husband and I were stuck making a much larger out-of-pocket investment than we expected. Though market conditions changed in the six months between signing the lease and getting bids for the buildout, my landlord was unwilling to budge.

The unknown of the increased costs to buildout nearly resulted in not opening the store. We met with the landlord to see if they'd be willing to cover the difference on the permanent elements and looked into lawyers who could advise on what our options were for getting out of the lease, despite not having an "out" clause other than subleasing. We were stuck with what we had.

I wanted the space. The space felt like a YES in so many ways. But if the landlord wasn't going to cover the true costs of the elements they left for the tenant to do, elements that were permanent parts of their building, then it wasn't going to be worth continuing.

To spend money on the bones of the place meant less for me to spend on the store design, merchandise, and ongoing operations. What was the point of having a great space if I couldn't afford to have displays to match, buy the right opening inventory, or hire the help I knew I needed? I didn't want to spend our money on running cables for electricity to our space or pouring a concrete slab to create a floor. I wanted to spend that money on enhancements to the store. I was in a holding pattern for purchases as we determined how much more we'd be willing to invest, financially and emotionally, in my dream if we moved forward. The store was set to open in several months, and it was a high-stress time.

We decided to keep building with the optimism that we'd have our full lease term, five years, to make a return on our investment. It was a good thing that my "shipping port" vision for the space was simple and allowed us to embrace the raw industrial elements that would remain, making the remaining build as cost effective as possible. It cost us an additional $30,000 out of pocket to pour the concrete floor, build the dividing wall, run the electrical (we were farthest away from the electrical room), and install the HVAC and sprinkler systems. These were all permanent building elements that the space required, the city required, and that we absolutely needed. Also, elements that I resented spending money on since I could never sell them off or take them with me.

And of course, there were hiccups. Expensive ones. Here were early opportunities to think creatively, like it or not. In particular, when it came time to install our telecom lines by connecting to a "stub" in the gravel floor, I was informed by our contractor that the appropriate lines had not been run from the building's main communication's box. The stub was not "hot" like I'd been led to believe, and it was going to cost $10,000 to 14,000 to run the lines from the other side of the building where the box was housed. After a freak-out moment—*How could I operate without internet?! We're not paying for that!*—my husband offered a brilliant solution: cellular data. We ran the entire store for five years from an iPad with a data plan, hot-spotting and Bluetoothing whatever and whenever we needed. That decision is one that I'm most proud of in terms of cost savings, problem solving, and pragmatism.

We had initially anticipated spending $50,000 to 60,000 in buildout costs, including the $30,000 TIA, but our total was just over $90,000 by the time we opened the store. It was a big blow. I had a frustrating experience trying to get a small business loan from local banks and credit unions. You can have the right types of credit and assets, and it still feels like they want you to sign away your firstborn child. We reluctantly accepted a $125,000 loan from my parents-in-law.

The family loan seemed crazy because I didn't grow up with family money as an option. Support of all other kinds, yes, but not cash. My husband didn't grow up with family money, either, but his parents were thrifty spenders, wise savers, and were pushing their eighties by that point. They were happy to support me, to support us, and I was grateful for the opportunity. The loan was initially intended to cover a small part of the buildout, opening inventory costs, and to provide a runway for operating expenses during the first year of business. I was excited to have a financial cushion to hire someone part time almost immediately. But having to spend that extra $30,000 on permanent elements of the building ruined that plan. The setback added to a hefty emotional toll from the start.

I held onto anger, disappointment, and frustration with the landlord for the first two years. Then I got tired of feeling that way and decided to get over it. The money was spent, and I needed to move on for my own peace of mind. Stewing on resentment wasn't worth my energy. *They* weren't worth my energy.

Your buildout reality can be different from mine.

If you choose a raw space, be it a new build or old warehouse, work with a broker who can ensure that permanent building elements are covered by the landlord. You want to use your valuable funds on *your* elements, your displays, decor, merchandise, and payroll. Research a buildout budget in advance of signing your lease by asking neighboring or similar businesses what costs they incurred to hire to architects, designers, carpenters, painters, and general contractors. You will find that most small business owners are happy to help out fellow entrepreneurs.

If you choose an existing space that's move-in ready, then you're already ahead of the game. No need to think about building interior walls for hanging your shelves or basics like pouring concrete to have a floor. You can jump right into the interior design elements and focus on how you'll tell a story through your merchandise and excellent customer service. Still, do your due diligence for necessary buildout costs. Even if the space is move-in ready, you can negotiate for a TIA.

If your Shopkeeper Dream must happen at *any* expense, let any spent monies be that: spent and in the past. Focus your energy on the present and future of your store, and don't let resentment or frustrations get in the way of the magic you create for yourself and your community.

Key Takeaways
→ Raw spaces are full of potential—And expenses. Be prepared.
→ Do your due diligence for anticipated buildout costs.

Take Inventory
→ How can you best prepare yourself for the financial investment of signing a lease? What mindfulness practices can you employ?
→ What creative solutions can you employ to meet your needs even when circumstances don't meet expectations?
→ How can you focus on the purpose of your buildout expenses rather than stress over having them?

PAY, ASK, GIVE

To launch and live out your Shopkeeper Dream, you will need to spend money and ask for help. Getting comfortable doing both, early and often, will only benefit you and your business.

Paying for professional help is often necessary to grow and thrive. We're not meant to do things alone all the time. For your business, there are professionals out there who can do a job better than you or just as well. More importantly, they have the dedicated time and focus to do it because it's their primary job. Unlike you. Some can save you money by helping you make smarter choices since they've 'been there done that'; their hard lessons are your gain. Others can give you more time and space to work your vision and do what *you* do best. Graphic designers, business advisors and coaches, bookkeepers, accountants, copywriters, window cleaners—they can all help you see more clearly and keep you in your flow.

My store always looked and felt better when its prominent nineteen-foot floor-to-ceiling windows were crystal clear. I cleaned them myself for the first three years, ladders and all. Occasionally, I would pay a man who rode around the neighborhood on a bicycle with a squeegee and bucket in hand looking for work. But sometimes our storefront would go dirty for too long, usually reflecting my personal energetic outlook, and giving the wrong first impression to new customers.

When I finally decided to regularly schedule and pay for professional cleaning (it wasn't nearly as much as I thought it would cost), everything looked and felt better more often. I wondered why it took me so long to take action (control, a negative money mindset, laziness, all of the above) since the results were always money, time, and energy well spent. It's as if I'd personally been walking around wearing smudgy and dirty glasses, unaware of how obstructed my vision was until I took out a cloth and wiped off the grime. By letting someone else take out the cloth to wipe off the grime for me, money flowed to them, and their business, and positive energy flowed back to me to make room for crystal-clear vision.

Whenever I got stuck in the web of lack and fear, I failed to see that money itself could be a wonderful exchange of energy. An exchange that I could actively participate in because ultimately, a retail store is a place where value is exchanged; valued money is spent on valued things. When I learned to value clean store windows and the positive energy that they brought, I also learned to value spending money for a professional cleaner's time and work.

Recognizing that help is needed comes first. Then comes *the ask*.

The ask didn't come easy for me. If asking for help was a favor, I'd often assume that my ask would be too big or too demanding of someone's time and energy. If the ask was a professional service with a price tag on it, I'd often delay the ask or not make it at all. The first scenario denied people the pleasure of helping someone, and we all enjoy being needed and helpful at times. The second denied people from being supported financially for the services they offer. Telling myself that I could do "xyz" if I put my own time and effort into it was just another way of resisting asking and paying for help. The upsides of this approach were usually negligible and unnecessarily frustrating and time-consuming.

When we give joy, we get joy. In this case, giving your time, resources, and expertise can be a win-win for you and your community. I know that the first two, time and resources, can be hard to come by at first but when fellow Shopkeepers and local nonprofit organizations come to you for support, consider what that could mean for all of you. If, like money, everything is energy and you exchange that energy for good, what might be possible?

While I did make charitable contributions for annual campaigns, disaster relief efforts, and donate products for charity raffles and auctions, I can't help but imagine the impact the store could have had if I'd built automatic charitable giving into our operations. I never missed our monetary contributions or gifts-in-kind once they were donated, and more benefits always came back to me in the form of positive energy.

In my first business—the accessories side hustle I started while working at TOMS and continued doing while serving as marketing director for the shopping center—giving was built in. From day one, a percentage of sales went to a local creative arts program for kids in low-income communities. The checks I wrote were tiny, but they reflected a simple commitment to something bigger than me and my bags. Not surprisingly, it was a time in my life that I felt very connected with my truest self. This was another way of participating in the commercial + community ecosystem that, sadly, I had forgotten, dismissed, or ignored as a Shopkeeper.

Lucky for you, my remembrance of these moments is a call for you to drop the fear and ego and to not hold back. Don't hold back from asking or paying for help when you need support. Don't hold back in giving to local organizations that resonate with your store's purpose, ethos, and community whenever possible. Don't hold back on taking actions that will bring you clarity, time, and headspace—even if it costs money.

We need to take moments to stop and take Personal Inventory and to metaphorically clean our lenses. Upon reflection, we're able see ourselves, and the world, for the beautiful truths that exist. Each time we go through this process, we will wonder, *Why did it take so long to clean, refresh, and take notice?* Just like I did with those dirty windows.

Key Takeaways

→ A retail store is a place where value is exchanged; valued money is spent on valued things.
→ Get comfortable paying and asking for help. You won't be able to do everything on your own.
→ Giving your time, resources, and expertise can be a win-win for you and your community.

Take Inventory

→ Do you readily pay for services that you need, or do you DIY? Why is that so?
→ What is your current comfort level in asking people for help? Personal or professional?
→ What local organization could you partner with or support? What could that "something bigger" be for your store's greater purpose? Or your purpose as an entrepreneur?

SET IT AND (DON'T) FORGET IT

Starting a business can be like getting a brand-new laptop. Your new toy is shiny, polished, and ready for big, important work or play. You select a fresh new wallpaper image, clean up the mess of a filing system you transferred from your old laptop, and launch with the best intentions of keeping your computer's desktop tidy—along with your mind and your operations. Then the inevitable happens. Your desktop becomes a cluttered mess: folders here and there, files outside of folders, screenshots you no longer need, files on top of files because they have nowhere to go but "up."

This happens because we don't put the proper systems in place early, if ever. And if we do, we don't make the time to work the systems. Instead of taking an extra ten seconds to file something away in the appropriate folder, or create a new one, we leave it in the abyss of our desktop, cloud, or downloads, haunting us until we get frustrated and waste time and effort in the future, sorting documents into the files where they should have been saved in the first place. Systems work, but only as much as we work them.

Just like a clean new desktop on a screen, the goal is to keep our physical workspace and mental space feeling organized, open, and limitless. What steps can you take to create, nurture, and thrive in your store's operational systems every day? How can you take the ten seconds necessary to work a system instead of creating ten minutes or hours of extra effort in the future?

For example, what would it look like to spend a few hours setting up your shop's books with an accountant to make accurate and up-to-date P&L reports available within seconds when you need them? When managing your stockroom, cash wrap, sales floor, and bathroom supplies, do you have a weekly reviewed checklist for necessities that are running low and need restocking? I had a checklist for our supplies and worked the system off and on. Naturally, the system worked well when it was worked. And not so much when left unattended. There was one system, however, that I can proudly say was worked daily and diligently at our store: the walk-in sheet.

Jamie couldn't believe what she was looking at. She was a marketing rep for a new door counter that used infrared technology and a web-based app to track foot traffic for retail stores of all sizes. Jamie had deeply researched her offerings and had many in-depth conversations with retailers. She had never seen a sheet like mine before. Our walk-in sheet was a unicorn, as she put it, and conceded that we did not need a high-tech version.

We didn't need a digital door counter because my team and I *were* the door counters. We printed a new Walk-in Sheet every month with dates and sales goals. People could be in the store for thirty seconds or thirty minutes, either way, a tally was marked to count them in the day's foot traffic totals. Our humble analog sheet, used since day one, was a way to gather data, see our growth, and make informed decisions for future buying and staff scheduling. What days did we need more team support? What days/hours tend to be the slowest? Busiest? What weekends and seasons were highest and lowest in sales? I even made notes of local events and weather activity that could impact the day's foot traffic, sales spikes, or sales slumps.

Tracking visitor counts was something that I learned while working at Nordstrom during my first two years of college. Except their sheet had more to do with fairness for the commissioned-based sales teams. As sales associates, we worked closely with individual customers, but sometimes a customer would just "walk up" to checkout without having been helped by anyone in particular. This prompted a tally mark next to the sales associate's name listed next on the Walk-up Sheet. This system ensured that everyone on the team got a chance to benefit from walk-up sales and eliminated any incentive to hover by the register to boost their numbers. This was wonderful on hectic days when we were less likely to be one-on-one with every customer between cleaning fitting rooms and putting clothes back on the sales floor.

When things got busy at PofR, we'd have less time to count and mark on the spot, but once we caught our breath, we'd always note our best estimate. As time went on, I tweaked the template to allow more space for more tallies. I smiled every time I did so. Creating more space meant our foot traffic and visitor counts were growing. I could flip through dozens of pages, each representing one month, and see how we went from three people on a random Thursday when we opened to sixty a few years later, small potatoes for some retailers but a big sack of excitement for me.

Tallies for visitors weren't the only thing that I enjoyed tracking. Every year, our sales goals got bigger, and most months, we met or exceeded them. Writing our daily sales goal was also a remnant of my time as an assistant manager in my department at Nordstrom, where we'd break them down every month based on last year's sales and projections to meet this year's department goals. While my store's numbers were in the three- to five-figure range each day versus Nordstrom's six figures, seeing the daily goals and actual sales next to our visitor count was informative and powerful. It was data I could use, and did use, effectively until it was time to close. Knowing what I know now, the only thing I would do differently is add a column for energy levels. What energy did I, the store, and the team have that day? How could that be improved for the next day, and the next?

Systems can help us manage, organize, and streamline whatever we want. If possible, set yours up early, when your store and operations still have that new desktop feel and when you're the most motivated to keep it uncluttered. Then work the systems so they can work for you.

Structures are helpful, too, especially when you have a team, or are preparing for one. In the lead up to my maternity leave, I created our *Team Book*. It was a PofR 101 and how-to. Everything came out of my head and went into an easy-to-reference binder that we kept at the cash wrap. From Point of Sale (POS) basics and troubleshooting, to key store contacts and how we processed and packaged online orders, it was all in the *Team Book*. Everyone on the team was as excited about it as I was, even if they'd been with us for a while.

A Master Vendor List also proved to be invaluable once I took the time to build and flesh it out. Each product vendor and brand we purchased from had different Terms & Conditions (T&Cs)

for reorders. They each had different minimum quantities, minimum order cost, special orders, custom orders, delivery timelines, and drop-shipping.

Since I was the buyer for the store, I kept track of these details in my head and in emails. This worked fine when I was the one helping a customer or was readily available for my team. But ultimately, my team needed to be empowered (and I needed a better point of reference than my emails) to look up vendor information. For example, if a customer wanted a floormat in a size that we didn't carry in the store—but we could order one from the vendor because they didn't have any reorder minimums—my team could quickly reference the Master Vendor List spreadsheet on our cash wrap's iPad and inform the customer that we could have the item shipped to their house or delivered to the store within five business days. This structure helped us serve our customers better.

Systems and structures are exciting, probably because they're so helpful. They provide clarity to the entire team and empower everyone to do their best work. As a Shopkeeper, there's so much to take note of that can affect your energy input and output, so set it and (don't) forget it. Set yourself and your team up to invite more ease and flow into your operations from day one, if not ASAP. This also applies to setting up a scheduled window cleaning service and the like!

Key Takeaways
→ Systems work, but only if you work them. Save yourself time and angst by setting them up and letting them support you.
→ Structures empower and expand your team's operational knowledge. Structures also liberate your team's reliance on you, the Shopkeeper, for relevant information.

Take Inventory
→ Think back to systems and structures you've used successfully in the past, your systems or those created by others. What might you replicate or adapt for your operational needs?
→ Do you readily follow through with systems and structures? Or do you find that you abandoned them more often than not? Why might that be?
→ What boundaries could you put in place, physiological and tangible, to ensure that you work your systems and let them work for you as much as possible?

BUY YOUR OPENING INVENTORY

Buying your merchandise may be the most climactic part of preparing to launch your store. It's fun but can also feel daunting. If you're new to retail buying, all you have to do is lean into your *why*. The reason you're opening your store, why you know something is worth sharing and why you're excited to share it with other people. Your why is the inspiration that guides your merchandise mix.

My inspiration came from the modern furnishings and experiences I had while living and traveling in other parts of the world. I wanted to be a part of redefining *modern* for the American market, starting with Raleigh and North Carolina. To me, that meant bringing in contemporary designs and brands from Europe, Scandinavian countries, and Japan that all shared a common language of simple yet impactful form and function. Not cold and sterile but delightful and playful, full of intrigue and, for the most part, useful over purely decorative.

Equipped with my *why*, I was prepared with thoughtful intentions and a plan of action as I stepped inside the grand Javitts Center near Hudson Yards in New York City. I felt like I had arrived. I had been to retail trade shows in the past, but *NY Now* was my first trade show as a retail buyer. I beamed with excitement and nervousness all at once as I waited in line to get my official badge while carrying a three-month-old Hazel on my chest. She and my husband came along because I was still nursing, and pumping breast milk was, unfortunately, something that my boobs refused to do well. The badge read: *Ana Maria Muñoz, Buyer, Port of Raleigh*. It was so official. I smiled the biggest smile as I walked over to my husband to share the cloud-nine moment. After a, "Yay, mama!" he took Hazel in his arms and off I went into the maze of booths and products, ready to start my duties as a retail buyer.

From having worked in retail, I understood how the buying and tradeshow ecosystem worked, but I was starting from scratch and portrayed more confidence than I actually felt. I had a basic list of home goods and lifestyle categories to fill and a budget, but everything else was up in the air. I didn't have the benchmarks of last year's sales, the knowledge of what sells well, or what *my* customers liked. I knew zip-zero-nada of that sort. I just knew what I liked and why I liked it. And I had to go with that.

One of the first booths I stopped at was a brand representative—they represent individual items from individual brands for you to buy; it's a like a micro-store for retail buyers. I was completely overwhelmed with all the choices, but not the buyer next to me. She was seasoned. I tried to act casual and browse nearby as I listened to her dictate her order to the brand rep without hesitation. I was so intrigued by her as I listened, "Give me twenty of the green, twenty pink, twenty blue, and oh yeah, we gotta have the yellow! Give me forty of those. Our gals love yellow."

Prior to that, I had haphazardly been making mental and written notes on the same cool Japanese mechanical pencils she was ordering, noting their price and trying to do quick summations to see where I landed. *Do I order four of each, ten of each? Can I afford ten of each? What colors do I even start with?!* I wanted to be that woman who knew that her customers loved yellow and didn't care what the total cost of the order was. She didn't care because she knew she'd sell them all. That woman was confident, decisive, and knew her shit. I could not wait to be her. I eventually did become her, and you will have so much fun being her, too, if you're not already.

My first buying trip was ultimately a thrill. Insecurities faded as I went from booth to booth and spotted designs that were immediate *YESs*. Shopping the tradeshow floor became a practice in trusting my instincts and surrendering to the process. A practice that I got better at and had more fun with every season.

For our opening season, PofR's merchandise was sparse due to the available budget. Yet the designs we launched with made a big splash with the people who were ready to receive them. Why? Because I knew my *why*.

Key Takeaways
→ Base your buying on your store's why. Within your budget, of course.
→ Enjoy the journey of becoming and being a confident, decisive, and know-your-shit buyer.

Take Inventory
→ What is your store's why, and how does that translate to merchandise?
→ How will you pair your budget with your expectations?
→ What personal beliefs (imposter syndrome, scarcity mindset, sense of self-worth) could you address before hitting the trade show floor or digital showroom?

PART IV
OPENING

CELEBRATE!

Your doors, or door if you're like most small shops, have opened to the public. The cash register is singing "ca-ching!" and you are both thrilled and relieved to be in this moment. It's time to party.

A grand-opening party is a trifecta event: a marketing opportunity, a way to thank everyone who's been on the journey with you, and a way to meet new people who are keen to join the fun. You can make the party as intimate or as public as you want, but make it happen ASAP because it can set the tone for what people expect from you and how you engage with your community.

I opened my store in December, the middle of the holiday season, and used that time to build momentum for our belated grand-opening celebration in January. My personal invite list was short, but our core customers had started showing up and shared the store with their people. I hired a DJ to set the celebratory mood, worked with a local chocolatier to offer PofR branded chocolates as special treats, and partnered with a soon-to-open neighboring bar and restaurant for the bar service. It was a fun night of connection, discovery, and shared enthusiasm. I felt so supported by the response, especially since 98 percent of the people were there to check out the store and welcome us to the community.

Making the time and effort to celebrate in a way that feels right for your store can be worthwhile. The sooner you start connecting with customers in a joyful way, the better.

Key Takeaway
→ A grand opening party is a trifecta event: a marketing opportunity, a way to thank everyone who has been on the journey with you, and a way to meet new people keen to join the fun.

Take Personal Inventory
→ What is your heartset's intention for a celebratory night?
→ Whom within your ecosystem, local businesses, and service providers, can you hire and collaborate with to create a memorable experience for all?

COUNT ON COMMUNITY

Your community is and will be everything.

From deeply rooted ties in the city where your store is based to personal affiliations with large and highly supportive groups like a church, the platform for your launch is instantly stronger when it's supported by an established personal network. Opening a retail store with a robust personal network can make all the difference in launch turnout and velocity. I saw this scenario play out time and again, and it is impressively consistent and reliable. Celebrating this network matters because the stronger and bigger your launching platform is, the more people you can reach with the news of your store opening. Your network will likely share your store with their network, thus increasing the overall number of people who are likely to support you early on and often.

But don't worry if this doesn't sound like your current reality. On my store's opening day, the head count of my personal community in North Carolina was around ten. My husband and I moved to Raleigh with zero contacts, friends, or family. The ten people with whom I shared the store's opening were neighbors turned friends, maternity fitness class comrades, and Instagram #newfriendsIRL. My organic support system and circle of people to instantly sell to was *tiny*.

What I didn't start with, however, I created through the store day by day. Prior to moving to Raleigh, I hadn't felt a major sense of community in many years. Having left my native network of friends, colleagues, and family in Los Angeles for London, then Kuala Lumpur, I spent the better part of the proceeding four years hanging out with my husband. Sure, I made friends, but it was not easy; it never is as an adult without the supporting context of life in an office and the like. But with PofR, I created a gateway to getting to know my family's new community and effortlessly made my friends. The store was a beacon of sorts for the people who were ready and excited to have it in their new, or native, hometown.

Count on your existing community, of any size, and build it as you go. You will grow together all the same.

Key Takeaways
→ Use your network to your advantage because it gives your new store a head start.
→ You will create and nurture your store's unique community, regardless of the initial size of your network.

Take Inventory
→ How comfortable are you in sharing personal and professional news with your network?
→ How will you share your store's news with your network, and how will it differ from person to person? Through social media, personal emails, texts, or phone calls?
→ Who are the people in your life that you know for sure, no matter where they are, will celebrate and share your news? Lean on them to expand your energy for those you have yet to meet.

FINDING YOUR PEOPLE

Your store's community will ultimately be made up of *your people*, your core customers. These are the people who are open and happy, even eager, to receive your store. Your audience size may vary depending on your immediate market area and the niche or wide appeal of your merchandise. Regardless, you can and will find an audience. You also won't be everyone's cup of tea, and that's okay—wonderful, even.

It's not for you . . . These four words of conviction shifted my perspective one year into running the store as I continued to get my bearings as a new mom and a business owner. Zero budget for paid advertising meant that I needed to be creative in my quest to get more people in town to take notice, care that we existed, and come in to experience what we offered.

The people who would become our loyal customers, community, and friends, took notice. They cared a lot and came to us as soon as they could, but I needed more of those people. Foot traffic was a slow trickle, and, if I wanted to grow my books and hire help anytime soon, I needed a divine downpour. My confidence was shaken as I began wondering if I had misjudged the local appetite for my retail concept. I knew a shift was on the horizon when a regional home show was scheduled to take place at the neighboring convention center. I was excited. This was it! Not only did we sell goods for the home, but our storefront would be passed by hundreds, if not thousands, of attendees who would park in our adjacent parking deck or walk across town. Finally, a steady stream of foot traffic!

To my disappointment, I learned that foot traffic doesn't equal curiosity. Very few attendees (I knew they were attendees because they all carried the same promotional tote bag) popped in to see what we had to offer, and even fewer made purchases. The majority of our passers-by stared straight ahead on their path, either oblivious of or unwilling to see that a store, my store, existed just to their right or left. Others slowed down with perplexed looks, wondering what the heck they were looking at from outside the window. I could interpret their stares as, *What is this place? What is that stuff?* To be fair, the store could have been mistaken for a gallery at the time. The large vinyl letters spelling "Design Store" and "Home, Lifestyle, Gifts" had not been added to our windows.

Eventually, a group of women who had just left the convention center came into the store. Correction: *one* eager woman entered and coaxed the rest of her party into joining her. While the eager woman matched my cheerful greeting and quickly walked toward something that caught her eye, her reluctant followers seemed to have stepped into invisible quick-dry cement by the door. They crossed their arms, gripped their bags against their bodies, and gave the impression that they smelled shit in the air. I want to believe that my memory exaggerates their reaction to my store, full of things I had personally selected and placed on shelves with love, but I remember the encounter so vividly. It was painfully obvious that these women were out of their element. Painful for them and painful for me to witness—but also so helpful for me to experience.

My store wasn't for them. They clearly preferred a different retail experience by way of different products, different design aesthetics, or different environments. They could have employed a little of the charm the South is so famous for, maybe just a polite smile, anything other than repulsion. But the eager woman who coaxed them inside? PofR was definitely for her, as it was for the subsequent people who chose to come in and shop with us that day and beyond.

Accepting that the store wasn't for everyone made a huge difference in my day-to-day expectations and in learning how to serve our core customers. These customers chose to shop with us year-round; they came to us for special occasions like birthdays, anniversaries, graduations, baby showers, or for everyday household needs and treats for themselves. Without the support of their dollars, we'd have had no business, and I am grateful for each and every one of them.

A Shopkeeper's Dream sets the vision and creates the time and space for anyone and everyone to explore and enjoy the same things they love. But it's the core customers who bring a retail store to life day in and day out. As a Shopkeeper, you will only get better at serving them your perfect cup of tea rather than worrying about the reactions of people for whom your store doesn't resonate.

Key Takeaways
- → It's not for you... These four little words will change your Shopkeeper life.
- → Core customers are open and happy, even eager, to receive your store.

Take Inventory
- → What expectations do you have for who your audience will be?
- → How can you be mindful of those who aren't your people and not take it personally?
- → How can you be reminded of your store's *why* daily to support you through vulnerable moments?

MIND YOUR ENERGY

Along with hanging your OPEN sign for all to see, what if you also hung a sign that read something like this?

"Please leave bad energy at the door."

This sign doesn't just serve as a request to guests venturing into your store, but as a reminder to yourself when entering your own creation. I once heard Oprah share that she posted a similar note on her dressing room or office door so that negative energy wouldn't drain the positive productivity she worked hard to cultivate.

Hearing this, I was reminded of a couple who walked into the store one day with a peculiar energy. No eye contact, not a word, and stiff as boards. They refused to acknowledge that my teammate and I existed. I understand that social comfort levels are different for everyone—and they may have been out of their element—but after they completed their awkward lap around the store and walked out the door, my teammate and I instinctively moved our bodies as if to shake off their vibe. The aura they entered with and left behind was so strange that I considered smudging the space to cleanse the energy. But alas, the scent of sage wasn't on-brand for us.

On the flip side, there were times when *I* created and left bad vibes in the store. When I didn't mind my energy and was negative, stressed, low, or not fully present, our guests felt it. They'd shop, linger, and engage less, possibly costing us a sale.

Early one evening, back from my maternity leave after my second daughter's birth and working alone, I believe I let two potential customers down. It was their first time in the store, and they walked in with excitement in their eyes. It had been a long but quiet day chipping away at a heavy load of new arrivals. After unboxing the new merchandise, adding items to our inventory system, and creating price tags, I was exhausted—mostly because I didn't want to be there. At the cash wrap, I was surrounded by towers of bath towels and boxes of kitchenware, waiting to be sorted in the backroom and merchandised on the floor. The store looked like a hot mess; frankly, so did I.

The two eager visitors were visiting specifically in search of a plant pot and stand that they'd heard we carried. My usual friendly and eager-to-serve demeanor was nowhere to be found as I showed them the details and we discussed the design. I wasn't rude, but my energy was clearly *meh bleh blah*. They decided that the plant stand was too small and said their goodbyes with a polite but seemingly unsatisfied smile. I could feel my heart drop as they walked out of the store. I had just given them a shit experience. The store's appearance and service matched my energy levels—physically, mentally, and spiritually—and, therefore, did not meet their expectations.

It hurts me to admit that when I wasn't feeling great, it also affected my team. I was in a *bad* mood one morning before opening the store. I had been away for several days and having left new merchandising up to the team, I arrived extra early to reacquaint myself with the sales floor. Next thing I knew, I was on my knees, rearranging things around on a shelf and cleaning up dust bunnies that were missed. I was annoyed and frustrated that I was doing the above because, well, I was in a mood. I heard keys jingle and my employee opened the door, ready to greet me with a smile. Before she could even say her first word, she saw me scrunching my face and talking to myself in a disgruntled manner. My bad-mood-energy was so visible and palpable that her expression immediately shifted from *Hello!* to *Ohhh Shit* in an instant. She quickly and cautiously wished me a good morning as she rushed to the back room to set her things down and start the day. We both carried on. She was the total professional that she had always been, and I got better but not my nearly best. This memory will forever be a teachable moment for me on how our personal energy can influence others in a heartbeat.

We might not actually hang a, *"Please leave bad energy at the door"* sign in our spaces, but the consideration, mentally or through a symbolic visual reminder, can be the invisible reminder to be kind and maintain positive energy.

In preparing to launch the store, I devoured a book about feng shui, written for retailers. Wherever possible, I implemented the book's teachings in the store, but the most memorable was the instruction to place a small hand mirror on top of the toilet to counter money being flushed down the drain, or something like that. The shiny object I selected to fill that role was visible and sparked curiosity and conversation by all who used our private bathroom. While a mirror on the toilet wasn't a visual cue to mind my *personal* energy, it was a step in a direction worth exploring... had I thought to.

Similar to the considerations I had when organizing the

store, I could have considered my own feng shui touchpoints for launching the next version of myself as a business owner. *What energies did I want to consciously bring to the table as a Shopkeeper and operator? What were my personal feng shui points to be mindful of, to tweak, to enhance, and to resolve? Where did I need to put a figurative mirror to counter negative energy?* Answering these questions and regularly tuning into myself could have been useful to catch and prevent bad vibes from being dragged inside through the front door. Because when I was good, everything felt great.

I wanted every day to feel like the day that Lauren, a fellow Shopkeeper, visited PofR. I had recently remerchandised the space, thoroughly cleaned it, and renewed my good energy and intentions. I was happy with the results; the store looked and felt superb. And not just to me. Lauren is someone with an incredible spirit who emits a loving and kind energy through her entire being. On that particular day, she walked around the store saying, "Man, it feels *good* in here," and waved her hands in front of her as if to flow with the energy she was feeling. Lauren's reaction meant a lot to me, and I understood what she felt. I always knew and felt when the store was in its sweet spot, and on that day, oooh, was it sweet.

I believe we can learn to bottle up this sweetness and bathe in it with the awareness that comes from taking personal inventory. The sooner you do it, the sweeter and more consistent the experience will be for you and all who support you. If the store is an expression of your vision, and its sensorial contents deliver the message, you must also consider how you're *being* through the energy you put out.

Key Takeaway
→ Personal energies can influence others in a heartbeat, for better or worse.

Take Personal Inventory
→ What daily reminder or ritual could you establish at the store to check your energy?
→ How might you communicate that reminder or ritual to your team?
→ What mental health tools or practices could you enact when you need support?

SHOW UP FOR YOUR TEAM

If you're fortunate enough to have an employee or a team—people you trust with your in-store and customer experience, and who trust *you* with their time, energy, and efforts as employees—then it's worth checking your energy every time you enter the door for a new business day.

Owning and operating a store by myself was exhausting and lonely at times. Even with customers to keep me company throughout the day, there was nothing like having people to commiserate with, scheme with, and celebrate moments of success with in real time. Someone you can trust with your business. I believe that I trusted my team but, years removed, I also believe that I held trust back.

Holding trust back kept me from delegating more when it came to marketing, buying, and visual merchandising—the three things I enjoyed most about shopkeeping. Or perhaps I always knew that the experience would be short-lived, so I didn't see the point of investing too much time and effort into replacing myself. There's always that notion, but it mostly seems like an excuse; a good leader leads and nurtures no matter the situation.

Throughout the store's lifespan, there were primarily two of us. I met my first employee on Instagram. We connected before she moved to Raleigh, and she came by the store as soon as she arrived in town. She became my right hand, sounding board, co-creator, and our "Let's give our customers a GREAT experience!" cheerleader. Her enthusiasm and sense of ownership was increasingly valued as we fleshed out the in-store experience and hired more part-time employees.

That whole your "vibes attract your tribe" thing played out for me. I was lucky that the right people always showed up for me at the right time. In the times when I most felt that I had "made it," there was a proper little team of three to five employees. Only once did I post a formal job announcement, resulting in a lot of *not-right-for-us* candidates. It did, however, give one core customer the impetus to express her desire to work with us. And of course, she was hired.

Every employee who joined us, for a little or a long while, was sent by the universe, even when it felt like I was struggling to ask for, and receive, help. They may never truly know how thankful I was for their presence and contributions. Though at times I wasn't in my best energies to be a boss, I was always grateful that they chose to work with me and for the store.

As the Shopkeeper, you set the tone for the day in how you show up for yourself and for everyone else. Show your team how much you value them by recognizing, valuing, and respecting your collective energies, and by expanding your trust in them.

Key Takeaways
→ Create a vibe that's so strong you can't help but attract your tribe, aka people you can trust with your business.
→ Return the favor by empowering them in different ways and showing up as the leader they need you to be.

Take Inventory
→ What type of leader do you desire to be? What steps, systems, and structures could support this?
→ How might you be withholding trust in your team?
→ What opportunities for engagement or responsibilities could help them feel more invested and empowered in their roles?

PART V
OPERATING

CREATING THE IN-STORE EXPERIENCE

Every decision you make in selecting furnishings, lighting, paint color, and of course, merchandise, has a significant impact on the experience you craft for your customers. The store is an expression of your vision, and its sensorial contents deliver the message.

Everything we engage with is an experience, and everything we did at PofR was to be in service of that notion. Our motto and mini manifesto, *Experience Your Everyday*, was an invitation to celebrate the objects in our lives that create both tangible and psychological value.

I wanted our in-store experience to be about intentionality. In being intentional about the things we choose to bring into our lives and homes, from different sources, we define their value. More value leads to less waste, higher respect, an appreciation for how we consume, and when done well, more joy. When bringing the vision for PofR to life, I leaned into this concept by curating products made in the United States, products with B Corp frameworks, and products with excellent design that were thoughtfully made throughout the world. Offering intentionality through merchandise selection is what contributed to our unique in-store experience.

Our customer experience was built both through the objects we shared and how we shared them. Merchandising played a huge role at PofR. As things sold and new products arrived on a nearly weekly basis, displays shifted around in small but necessary ways. The real merchandising magic happened when the seasons changed, or a new month called for a holiday feature. I loved creating themes based on what products we had or would be ordering. The colors and textures, the visual dance of objects paired side by side; I still love thinking about it. I loved stepping back and squinting my eyes to imagine where things would go. I loved making the first move, the first shuffle that got the merchandising mojo going. I'd rarely put music on, preferring the silence of the practice which often included my small team (then we'd have music). Mostly, I loved doing it alone. It was my personal Zen, my time to play and create.

Merchandising sets the scene for a store. It influences the tone and pace and determines how fast or slow things will sell. It is part of your store's personality, and if you're a small retail business owner and do your own merchandising, it's also part of your personality. It certainly was mine. Sure, there are best practices for merchandising to create the most impact and success, yet there's something about the free-flowing creative expression that merchandisers take on that resonates most for me. As a customer, you feel it when you walk into a store. Engaging visual displays will always communicate where you are, why you're there, and how the store can serve you.

Good displays don't have to be visually pleasing to be effective, depending on the intention. Stepping away from the small retailer world for a second, consider Dollar General, a low-cost warehouse of sorts, versus Nordstrom, an up-market department store. As a customer, your expectations for the merchandise inside each store and how it's displayed are very different prior to stepping through the door. The store managers know this and merchandise accordingly, creating the experience their customers expect. I appreciate the strategy and continuity involved in national retailers' merchandising strategies, but my heart sings for the artful approach of boutique settings. It's where, to me, shopping feels more personal—where the store's merchandiser gets to play and, in return, so do their customers.

Merchandising can create magic for *everyone*, and at PofR, we meant everyone. From children to grandparents, our store was a place of engagement, discovery, and maybe even enchantment. A place where curiosity met delight, and where hands-on exploration was encouraged by adults and kids alike. Parents were thankful, I was happy for the fun playful energy, and the kids were generally well-behaved when left to their own devices. In five years, I personally broke more things on the sales floor than anyone else. In five years, only one kid broke something by backing into a table too quickly, just an $18 sand hourglass. No big deal. Nothing was too precious in the store.

My own kids were often there "merchandising" and playing too. Hazel, my eldest, became a part of some customers' experiences, leading to their disappointment when they'd visit and she wasn't there. She was indeed the cutest little Shopgirl, showing people her favorite items and making them "cards" using the yellow stickie notes and pens we kept at the cash wrap. She could also be found playing outside the storefront, drawing with chalk on the sidewalk, or sweeping fallen leaves away from our entrance.

For the first couple of years, unlike Hazel, I was there constantly. My being there became a part of our customers' experience. We'd share stories, talk about life, and geek out over *this over here* and *that over there*. When I finally hired part-time help, I was placing a new face in the store. It was evident that some returning customers were expecting to see me and looking forward to it. As reported by my team, these customers' faces would go through the stages of disappointment and acceptance within nanoseconds of walking in and seeing someone else. Fortunately, this subsided over time as people got used to all of us instead of *one* of us.

We strived to offer a positive customer experience for every visit. We did this in many intentional ways, from watching for dust bunnies during daily rounds of dusting and sweeping, to only burning candles and incense that we sold so when customers fell in love with the fragrance, they could take it home right then and there. Each consideration and touchpoint created our vibe. As will yours.

Key Takeaways
→ The store is an expression of your vision, and its sensorial contents deliver the message.
→ Good, engaging visual displays will always tell your customers where they are, why they're there, and how the store can serve them.

Take Inventory
→ How do you want to make your customers feel when they step into your store? What sensorial content can deliver that experience?
→ What parts of your personality come through in your merchandising? How can you apply merchandising fundamentals while staying true to your own magic?
→ If you're a part of your customer's experience, what does that mean to you, and how do you expand that to your team?

PLEASE PRESS PLAY

We can't talk about vibes and the in-store experience without talking about music. Music is a universal language and a big part of the way we experience social settings. This is why it pains me to walk into a retail store, cafe, or restaurant and hear nothing but silence. Silence is for libraries. If calm Zen is what you want to offer, there are endless ambient sounds for that. If you're at a loss for what to play, consider a music service provider that personally curates or uses AI to create your perfect playlist. Whatever you do, I beg you to enhance your in-store experience through intentional soundscapes.

Music was on from opening to close at PofR, and we had a dedicated playlist for each season. Since our only internet connection was the data plan on the store's iPad, and it was connected to multiple Bluetooth devices (printers, laptops, speakers, cashbox, to name a few), streaming music wasn't a good option. But that was okay because I loved creating playlists for the store. Our customers often took notice, commenting that they enjoyed the soundtrack to their shopping experience. If I missed the mark, they'd silently signal through body language or facial expressions. Thankfully it was nothing that hitting "Next" couldn't fix, followed by "Delete."

My favorite musical experience offered at PofR (second to our holiday season playlist) was one of the last playlists I created before closing the store. I called it Bossa Nova Sunday. On a random Sunday at home during the pandemic shutdowns, I played bossa nova music all morning and it felt *great*: light, uplifting, and easy breezy. It was a simple experience that brought my entire family joy. I brought that experience into the store as soon as we reopened late that spring. Visitors responded just at enthusiastically, and it was precisely what we all needed.

Your store is where your vision comes to life, and every detail deserves consideration for the customer journey. From merchandising to music, everything is an experience, and every touchpoint counts. It may not be perfect 100 percent of the time, but you can certainly strive for excellence and course correct as often as necessary. Give yourself permission and grace to adjust as you go.

Key Takeaway
→ Music is a universal language and a must for the in-store experience.

Take Inventory
→ What type of energy do you want to evoke in your store? What soundscapes could achieve that?
→ Do you believe investing time, energy, or money into curating your store's soundtrack is worthwhile? Why or why not?
→ How might you consider the time of year, time of day, or the day's weather before pressing Play?

BE OF SERVICE ONLINE

Having an online store for your brick-and-mortar is so easy and so wonderful and should not be taken for granted. Not one bit.

I think back to my college retail project and remember adding a $10,000 line item in the startup costs for hiring a web developer, the only way to create a proper e-commerce site at the time. Today, there are bountiful ways to start an online store with premade templates on prehosted websites already preset for Search Engine Optimization (SEO), starting at $30 per month, or even for free. There's often no web development necessary, no connecting to a separate web host, no tinkering around to add code for any purpose at all. Technology and all the tools and services that come from it let small mom-and-pop shops play big.

Selling online was part of my plan from day one, but it took over a year to launch digitally. It was a lot of work for one person, with a baby, working on it at night, after a long day working at the brick-and-mortar store. Starting an online store doesn't have to be *hard* work; like I said, the available technology and services make it easy. It does, however, involve a lot of redundant detail-driven work that can feel never-ending when you're in the thick of it. Once you're up and running, the redundancy of adding new products and managing inventory gets easier and faster to work through. The workload spreads out and is no longer all-consuming, and it becomes a part of your routine and flow.

The work was well worth the effort because I considered our e-commerce store a service to our customers. Browsing with us online let our audience engage with us on their terms—wherever, whenever. I found that many of our local customers browsed our website prior to coming into the store. I knew this from talking with them but also because I'd often see their abandoned shopping carts in the store's dashboard and, within a week, they'd walk through the door. Not only did these customers buy what they had abandoned in their digital cart, they typically bought more, finding items they had missed on the website. The in-store experience naturally led to more discovery.

Having an online store to share with our out-of-town visitors proved to be fruitful as well. It felt incredible to be thought of by travelers who chose to continue shopping with us once they returned home. Especially if they lived in major cities where the choices for shopping are plentiful.

PofR's hands-on sensorial and personable in-store experience was our customers' first and foremost method of shopping with us, but they also appreciated the convenience of gathering information and planning their purchases without having to step foot in the store.

Remember, I'm a customer, too, so while the following is a big-store example, it speaks to embracing e-commerce in independent retail . . .

It was pouring rain, a late-summer storm. I was sitting in our parked car in front of REI while my husband and eldest daughter were inside buying a rain jacket for her. Prior to driving to the store in the rain, we checked out their website to view the options and ensure they had one in stock. A man dressed in Birkenstocks with socks, cargo shorts, and a T-shirt under an unzipped rain jacket walked out of the store holding an umbrella in one hand and three pairs of new socks in the other. He seemed very satisfied, like he had completed a mission to buy those socks. He could have purchased the pairs of socks online and had them delivered to his home, either from REI's website or the hundreds of other online stores that carry the same brand and style of socks. But he didn't. He decided that he wanted or needed those socks ASAP, rain or shine, and that he would get them from REI's physical store, a place where he could touch the socks and perhaps compare and quickly scan all the options hanging on display versus clicking through digital images. Perhaps he, too, had shopped REI's website before driving to the store to make his rainy-day mission a guaranteed success through either an in-store purchase or their click-and-collect option. Whether or not my story about this customer's journey was true, REI's online store was likely a customer service tool for at least a few of us on that rainy day.

Few Shopkeepers are able to get away with sustainable or thriving sales without having an online store, or at the very least, a modern website that shares relevant information and entices people to come to your store. However, well-established retailers who are already at or past their ten-year anniversary mark have proven longevity and loyalty, and niche retailers who sell unique-to-their-market goods such as vintage clothes, antique furniture, or hard-to-find brands are more likely to keep customers coming in, despite having no web presence. If your store doesn't fall into these two categories, then you need to sell online or at least have a modern website. Don't fall into the common trap of assuming that a Facebook or Instagram profile will reach everyone or appear professional enough to convince those who do see your profile to come to your store. A website is the most accessible way of sharing what you have and what you do beyond your brick-and-mortar's opening hours.

Selling exclusively within four walls is every small retailer's prerogative. I was honest with what that meant to me and knew that my only competitive advantage was my personal POV, passions, and curation, all of which created the specific experience we offered to our customers in-store. Yet despite how hard I worked to carry unique things, I knew that our current and potential customers, local or not, would be likely to find exactly what we sold in another online store, regardless of the in-store experience. So why not carve out a place online and make it easy for customers to support us? Our people wanted to support us and were happy for the e-comm option.

Physical retail stores will always hold a different value proposition for shoppers than e-commerce. But your customers' time is valuable, as are their expectations. You can, and should, set your store up for a solid presence to meet your audience wherever they may be and however they may want to engage with you, online and offline.

Key Takeaways
→ Creating and managing an online store is easy. Don't take the accessibility and affordability for granted.
→ Your e-commerce store can be a service to your customers.

Take Inventory
→ How are you using the available e-commerce tools to your business advantage?
→ Are there any website-related opportunities you might be holding off on due to subconscious blocks like lack of time, confidence, or money?
→ What would having 10 percent of your sales come through e-commerce mean to you and your store? How about 20, 30, 40 percent, and so on? What would this look like operationally?

LIFT ALL [BRANDS] BOATS

In our brick-and-mortar storefront, I happily shared the names of the designers and brands we carried. When setting up our online store, I had to decide if I would do the same. Online felt different. Online wasn't the same container of experience that walking into the store was. Online had all the competition in the world at customers' fingertips. But if a rising tide lifts all boats, then noting our brands was the way to go.

I studied what my peers did with their online stores. Some presented products and included the designer and brand name, while others chose to forego that information and simply offered a generic product name by description—"blue stool," for example, "a stool you can sit on." The latter always felt a bit disingenuous, at least for me. Not because I thought that these retailers were trying to trick their customers and pass on designs as their own, but because so much of why I started the store was about celebrating small independent brands and designers. By not sharing the brands and designers' names with our customers online, I felt I would be doing everyone a disservice. I also knew that I'd be missing out on valuable SEO that could boost organic visits to our webstore and drum up interest for our brick-and-mortar.

Some retail peers likely kept product brands and designers to themselves to protect their sources, unique curation, and their perceived, or actual, exclusivity. With the digital landscape being what it is and other retailers comparing and competing with like stores, merchants who introduce brands into their market first risk revealing their sources to their competition. It's understandable that small retailers would find subtle ways to keep their offerings unique.

In choosing to share our brands and designers online just as I shared in person, I boosted our online sales through organic web traffic for specific brands and products. It was satisfying to receive an online sale like this because it meant that we offered someone exactly what they were searching for in a sea of information and offerings. Even more rewarding was when the purchased item was something that I'd spent a lot of time sourcing to become the first retailer to carry the item in either North Carolina or the US. The internet helped us spread the love.

As the years passed, I saw major retailers pick up the small independent brands that I introduced to the Southeast US, brands that just a handful of other small shops around the country previously represented. As the simple and modern aesthetic I shared became more widespread, more independent, corporate, brick-and-mortar and online stores began to carry and celebrate the same small brands and designers we launched and grew with. The pendulum swing was inevitable, and I took it as a bittersweet compliment. Here was proof that the design aesthetic PofR sought to celebrate did have a place in the American market.

Choosing to actively share our products' brands and designers was ultimately the right choice for our store. More importantly, our brands appreciated it. Emerging independent designers and brands need name recognition so they can grow. Larger established brands deserve to be recognized and continue to grow too. I saw it all as another mini ecosystem, one between the designers, makers, sales reps, and the stores that sold their goods. Of course, there were days when I wanted to claim ownership of our tiny part in getting a specific design or brand out there. *We* (I!) took the chance first. *We* contributed to a new aesthetic movement! But all of that was ego, not business. It's a win-win at the end of the day. When you support your designers and brands, you support your bottom line, not to mention your mission. You may even create positive ripples in your industry.

Key Takeaways
→ Celebrate and share your store's brands and makers. The recognition circles back to you.

Take Inventory
→ What are your views on "a rising tide lifts all boats"?
→ If your curated merchandise is no longer unique or exclusive to you, how might you check your ego against your values and your store's mission?
→ What brands and designers could you partner with to cross-promote authentically?

Operating | Lift All [Brands] Boats

portofraleigh

During their talk at Hopscotch Design Festival, Natalie and Mayela of Good Thing talked about their relationship with retailers – stores like Port of Raleigh that sell their wares in-person, around the world – and why it matters to them.

And on Friday night during our event with Good Thing, I witnessed the one-on-one interactions between people that can only happen in a brick & mortar space like ours.

We don't just sell things. We are a place where our community can gather, meet, engage, and share with one another. The things we share in our space, created by passionate people who believe that good design makes our world better, brings us all together. Port of Raleigh is still new and small, and our dreams are still so big. But with every person who comes through the shop doors, we see our hopes for our city come to life more and more. We love growing with you, Raleigh.

SEPTEMBER 17, 2017

Add a comment...

MAINTAIN YOUR MERCHANDISE MOJO

You've been selling through items, testing, learning, and growing with your audience. And if you're reading the room right—observing your customers, sales data, business expenses, energetic output, and input—your merchandise mix and services will be an ever-evolving constellation. In this evolution you must keep your North Star in view: why you started the store, what you share, and how you share it.

Ask yourself the following questions: *Do the items on your sales floor reflect your original intentions? Has your merchandise strayed so far to appease or attract new customers that the original shoppers see less of what drew them into your store? Where have you prioritized margins, and where is there opportunity for higher markups? What are your customers asking for that you are not offering them, but could? What products feel like the essence of your store? Are these "essence" items also your best sellers?*

Maintaining the essence of the store is key. Here's an analogy I learned from a marketing consultant during my time at TOMS: When we drink coffee, the aroma is part of the experience. We hold the mug up to our lips, inhale through our nose, and proceed to take a sip . . . tasting what our sense of touch, sight, and smell just experienced. That smell is part of the coffee's essence, and we come to recognize it and love it. Substitute tea or hot cocoa here if coffee isn't your thing. In a similar way, your store has its own essence beyond burning incense sticks and candles to set the sensorial experience. Your store's essence is what people come to know about, delight in, and expect from your store.

Launching the store with YES items got us started, but over time I lost confidence that the market would match my enthusiasm. I began to prioritize products at sweet-spot price points (ours ranged from $28 to $36) over YES pieces that were higher ticket items or took up more shelf or floor space than other products. I believe that this diluted our essence and held our merchandise mix back from its full potential. Though I would keep products with my YES qualities at the forefront (functional, modern, simple, fun), these sweet-spot items would distract me from the type of designs that I found incredibly exciting to share; therefore, easy to sell, regardless of their price point. I slowly adopted the belief that, because I was in a small market, I couldn't be wholly unique *and* have the kind of sales and cashflow we wanted and needed. This was a total cop-out for losing sight of my North Star. It made me feel insecure and not as lit up as I once felt. And what helps sell your products more than anything else? You being LIT UP about what you're sharing!

After customers see you lit up—your bright energy paired with true intentions and delivery on quality—you may get asked, "What else can you show me?" This inquiry can be for different categories of merchandise that you haven't considered. Or perhaps have considered but don't think you have the audience for it. For me, apparel and dog products were often brought up. Interested parties liked what they saw in the store by way of homewares and personal accessories, and they trusted that they'd like what we'd share with them for their wardrobe and for their dogs.

Don't do what I did, which was nothing. I had my reservations about going into apparel and pet accessories, but they were unfounded. Drop the ego, leave money fears behind, and consider investing in new merchandise categories that will delight your existing community and attract new members. There's always an opportunity to listen to your customers and give the people what they want—infused with your store's essence.

Key Takeaways
→ Keep your North Star in view: why you started the store, what you share, and how you share it.
→ Your store's essence is what people come to know about, delight in, and expect from your store.

Take Inventory
→ What products align with your store's North Star? What is their sell-through rate?
→ Have you been making compromises with your merchandise buying? If so, what are they and why? If these choices have felt lackluster, how might your subconscious blocks be influencing these decisions?
→ How are you listening to your customers and delivering on their desires? How might you infuse your store's essence into the new products and categories that they're looking to you for?

WHAT ELSE CAN YOU SERVE?

Your customers may respect your taste and trust you so much that they ask about services. Services complement and go beyond the physical merchandise that you have for sale. A clothing boutique might evolve to offer personal styling sessions or seasonal wardrobe consulting, an art store might offer art classes, and a gallery may offer private art advisory. You can charge a lot more for a service than a coffee mug or throw pillow, and it can be a competitive advantage in your market.

You and your team likely already advise and consult on your core competencies freely, so your trusted expertise and opinion are why people go to you in the first place. But there's a difference between helping an in-store customer through their purchasing journey and extending that service beyond your four walls through an intentional package.

It didn't take long before people began to ask if I offered interior design services. I liked to say that I was open to the idea because I often fantasized about being an interior designer. But mostly, I worried about the time and energy it could take to create, manage, nurture, and execute a new business direction on top of the many unknowns I already faced as a new Shopkeeper. Even more, mama to a toddler.

Within a year of opening my store, a woman who would end up becoming a close friend was ready to expand her world and invited me to consider expanding mine. She was finally going to pursue her dream to work as an interior designer. We met for smoothies and she shared a thoughtfully written proposal for how we could join forces. Her local contacts and dedicated time during a work sabbatical, plus my store with its growing presence, industry connections, and local reputation for the type of modern and playful designs we both loved were a perfect combination.

One might consider this a lucky break, had I been ready to receive it. I passed on the opportunity almost as soon as the conversation started. Instead of talking about possibilities or asking her questions about her vision for us as partners, my excuses came from a place of fear. I feared jumping into a new direction with someone who I was just getting to know, and again, my perceived available time and energy to work on something else. My excuses felt valid at the time, but fear always blocks curiosity. Had I led with curiosity, I may have explored and accepted a potentially fun and fruitful opportunity with someone who shared my taste, enthusiasm, and passion for design. Not to mention a partnership that would make launching and operating a service-based revenue stream much easier.

A more present and open version of myself might have better appreciated what she envisioned for the both of us. She saw something in me and in my store that I was afraid to see in myself, for myself. It's as if I was trying to snuff an energetic spark. A more present and open version of myself might have said, "Let me think about it," and taken the proposal home to better digest the details instead of offering an immediate. "Thanks but no thanks". It was one of many lessons in realizing how I may have unintentionally blocked lucky breaks that came my way.

The experience with my friend left me curious about when and how I would take on interior design gigs, because I did want to do them. I eventually said YES to an inquiry from a couple who wanted help with a few furnishings and rooms in their home. I took the opportunity to work in tandem with my husband, who has a way with spatial planning and creative boldness. It was fun and I immediately recognized the value that the service could bring to our customers, our bottom line, and my expanded horizons. I did it once more for personal friends but never launched it as a proper service for our community.

As much as I enjoyed the creative side gigs, the time it took away from my family in the morning and evening hours made it difficult for me to see how I would grow it without having more staff support at the store. Yet again, I got tripped up in assuming it couldn't work due to the time and effort required in addition to operating the store. Imposter syndrome was also present in thinking that I didn't have what it took to call myself an interior designer (read: have proper credentials) even though I knew how to play the part. Maybe interior stylist was more fitting?

Had I taken personal inventory at that time, I might have discovered the limiting beliefs that kept me from leading with curiosity and playing with expansiveness. Had I seen the opportunities for what they were—creatively fulfilling and value-added ways to bring additional revenue to our books—then I could have found ways to make it all work. Just like I did with starting the entire store from scratch in a new hometown with a baby on the way, construction surprises and all.

Becoming a full-blown interior designer or stylist may not have been in the cards for that season of life, but expanding the store's offerings through interior services would have ultimately been more fun than work, a satisfying form of creative expression. Additionally, the work would have been in service of the store's purpose: *to support people's everyday experiences in the interior spaces they spend time in.*

Excuses are easy to come by, but I'm confident that if you're keen, you can find a service or offering that's a natural extension of what you already do. And find a way to do it. From consulting to hosting workshops or lectures, you can create additional value for your customers by sharing your expertise and interests in different ways. It's also a way to satisfy *Your Energetic Spark*™. Get curious and stay open to growing your income and impact.

Key Takeaways
→ Services complement and go beyond the physical merchandise that you have for sale.
→ Services can offer value to your customers, add to your bottom line, and expand your horizons.

Take Inventory
→ Are you noticing energetic sparks to create and offer a service, but you're suppressing them for reasons unknown?
→ What is actually true? Can you pause to get curious about the implications and possibilities of a complementary business opportunity?
→ What would make it possible to say *YES* to offering a service you know could add value for all involved?

SELL YOUR OWN PRODUCTS

When people like what you curate, chances are that they'll like what you *create*. When you share something with your logo on it, or design something unique for your store, you expand the opportunity for brand loyalty, affinity, and authority. You can also make better margins as your own wholesaler. From a custom-scented candle made in collaboration with your favorite candle maker to a private label clothing line sourced from a respected apparel supplier, creating and selling this way can also be a form of playing in and supporting the community + commercial ecosystem. If only I had heeded this advice, or rather, my hunch.

I was aware that offering my own designs and branded products could be a fruitful and fulfilling thing to do because I saw examples of other shops doing this successfully. Some offered jewelry they made in-house, throw pillows with curated fabrics made by local contract sewers, and clothing selected from private label suppliers with the shop's logo on the clothing tags. I was always impressed by the Shopkeepers who made all of that happen on top of their everyday duties. Technically, I knew how to create my own products, too, but energetically . . . that was a different story.

One of our most consistent best sellers were the Japanese mechanical pencils that I obsessed over during my first buying trip in New York. Knowing this, I wanted to offer PofR branded wooden pencils that were high-quality, made-in-USA pencils with a classic look. I wanted to give people the opportunity to just buy a pencil (you'll understand why later). I let my curiosity lead me, started research, but then stalled because I got busy running the store and prioritized placing orders on other products. When I revisited the idea, I asked for help from one my employees. She browsed online and took notes on available options during particularly slow days in the store. The concept started to feel doable, but I ultimately never got around to placing an order.

Perhaps it was the Minimum Quantity Order (MQO) that seemed overwhelming, or the price point attached. Whatever the reason, I was not clear and decisive, or energetically aligned, with what I wanted, so it never came to be. The sad thing is that I know now, perhaps even knew then, that those pencils could have been one of our best sellers. They would have been fun to offer and easy for people to buy and enjoy. A simple pencil would have made a good margin. My fear and distraction got in the way of what was possible.

If you have the idea for a unique product offering, then it's worth exploring. After you've considered the applicable details and the idea still feels good and worthwhile (the *why* and the numbers, your *qualitative* and *quantitative*), then don't let yourself get in the way. Think of it like this: if you're willing and able to place similar sized and priced orders with your wholesale vendors (as was my case), why wouldn't you be willing to place an order for your own product(s)? Why not place a bet on yourself and your vision? Every piece of merchandise you order for the first time is a gamble, so you might as well bet on yourself and your vision. You never know, perhaps your unique design is such a hit that you offer it wholesale to other retailers to share with their community.

Lean into curating *and* creating the merchandise for your store. You might even find that your creativity and additional revenue stream will blossom.

Key Takeaways
→ Selling your own products expands the opportunity for brand loyalty, affinity, and authority.
→ Bet on yourself and your vision for sharing wholly unique-to-your-store products.

Take Inventory
→ What brands or makers could you collaborate with for mutually beneficial product launches?
→ What type of custom or private-label products could be fun for you to design, source, and share? Why these items?
→ How might introducing your own products positively impact your store? Your sense of creativity?

TRADE IN TRUST

Every product we sold built trust. Every conversation my team or I had with our customers built trust. Did we get it right every single time? No. But every positive thing we did and shared, over time, built trust.

We extended trust to our customers in big and little ways. For example, we sold doormats that were available in a wide range of colors and patterns. We had sample swatches for all the options, and people often deliberated pretty intensely over their final decision: *Do we play it safe with the solid heathered grey or go bold with the striped multicolor?* Noticing this, we'd offer them the swatches to take home so they could better coordinate with the hues and tones of their front door or porch paint color. We could live without the swatches for a day or two. And our customers were happy for much longer than that.

People showed trust in us too. It meant the world whenever we received an online order with a gift message. It meant that the buyer trusted us with their gift-giving. They trusted that we'd send the recipient something well-packaged, on time, and with love.

Our community's confidence in what we had to offer was nurtured through our product knowledge and general enthusiasm.

For example, I ordered samples from first-time vendors to ensure that they were up to par before placing an order; simply looking good wasn't enough. When I didn't do this, I almost always regretted it, and we'd usually put the items on clearance, send them all back, or donate them to local charities (perfectly functional items but not right for us). I once sent back dozens of carbon-infused toothbrushes made in Japan. I thought they'd make a great addition to our growing category of bathroom accessories, but they were not a good fit. After using one of the toothbrushes once, my teeth became ultra-sensitive for days. This may not have been everyone's experience, but it was mine, and I couldn't in good faith speak positively about the product. I had to be 100 percent behind what we sold.

Because the items we sold and the stories we told were based on trust, we very rarely had returns. Online returns were almost nonexistent, and in-store returns were most often exchanges from gifts received. Our customers came to trust our taste, our voice, and our approach to care and details. Establishing this trust through what and how you share is just as important as the confidence your customers reflect back to you.

Key Takeaways
→ Your customers will come to trust your taste, your voice, and your approach to care and details.

Take Inventory
→ What does trading in trust mean to you?
→ How can you build trust into your product offerings and everyday customer service?
→ What boundaries or criteria can you enstate to maintain the trust you've created?

SHARING, NOT SELLING

Marketing, at its core, is sharing information with other people. Whenever I shared what I was excited about—new arrivals, a featured artist, or a product feature—I was never selling. Sharing on behalf of PofR occurred through multiple marketing channels where our people opted in to receive my content. No spamming, just sharing. This approach to what we sold and how we engaged with our people made marketing enjoyable.

Like many of you, my primary method of marketing was through Instagram and newsletters—they're both free or low-cost and readily accepted. Having used Instagram since its launch, I was very comfortable with the platform. Because in the early days, I was in the store all the time and sharing what I was excited about, I became the default face of the store. I initially wanted to keep business separate from my personal life, but I got used to posting Stories and photos of myself and, on occasion, my family; I needed to let people know what and who PofR was, what we offered, and why we existed. Since that worked in-store, I felt compelled to show up on social media in personable ways. Showing who you are and giving your customers excellent service and attention really works.

I put 90 percent of my marketing eggs into Instagram, which worked well for the store, but I was ultimately too personally tied to it. If the goal was to have the store be managed by other people day to day, then being the face of the business didn't work in the long run. However, transitioning out of the solo way of doing things and relinquishing social media to my team was tough. My "face" aside, I had created the brand voice in how I spoke and wrote and how I took photos and edited them. PofR and I were intertwined, and a part of me enjoyed it.

Creating your store's brand through your point of view and expression is fine, but there comes a time when you may need to hand things over for a while or even permanently. For example, I had to get everything out of my head and onto paper before my maternity leave. I created an Instagram style guide for our team to follow so that we'd have consistency in posts, yet I worried about our audience noticing changes in our style and tone during my absence. It stressed me out to think that any momentum I had built with our Instagram audience was at risk of slowing or faltering. It was hard to surrender my creative work, and I micromanaged posts when I didn't need to.

Beyond a style guide, I needed to create more trust. Trust that my team could do it all as well as I could, if not better, because they were also reflections of the store. More trust was crucial because we worked side by side, co-creating the in-store experience. We often shared ideas and creative expressions. The times when I didn't stressfully micromanage our social media marketing and visual merchandising, I experienced the joyful realization that the business could survive just fine without me physically or digitally present. It felt productive, uplifting, and next-level; these moments made me feel like a true boss. I didn't have to be the only face and voice behind the business.

The remaining 10 percent of my marketing energy was allocated to email marketing. The percentage doesn't reflect it, but I enjoyed putting time and effort into our monthly newsletter. I loved writing a short message to our community and curating the featured products around a seasonal theme or announcement. Our emails were a way to put PofR into a pretty package every month, offering information that people chose to receive directly to their inbox. I relished the pace and intention of sharing this way.

However, sending a promotional email more than once per month could have been better marketing. I used our newsletter to stay connected with our core customers beyond social media. It wasn't until the end of the store's life that I considered the total value of email data. Emails have much more power than many of us realize. Getting into people's personal (or even promotional) inboxes is infinitely better than hoping they pass you on their social media scroll. Every time I sent out our monthly newsletter, we had an average online order of $250 within the hour, directly from that email. I'm confident that each newsletter led to in-store sales within one to three weeks of delivery since our core community liked to visit us online and in-store frequently and often. Here was my example of how to do marketing without being the face of it—marketing that was extra joyful for me, effective, and worth the effort.

The instant ROI from our newsletter made my Instagram efforts look less appealing over time. I'll never deny the daily impressions from Instagram that supported ongoing sales in-person and online; we counted on them. But compared to emails, the social platform required a lot more effort for less concrete returns on investment. We only ever made one direct sale through Instagram's "shop tag" feature and sponsored posts. The joy and flow I experienced in creating each newsletter were energetic sparks that I converted to sales. Sparks that I could have used to create more frequent, intentional messages to share with our community.

Find what form of marketing aligns best with how you enjoy sharing, the strengths of your team, and your desired ROIs. If you want to be the face of your store, go for it. Use your extroversion to your advantage to support your brand and merchandise. If you prefer to let the store and your products do all the talking, that's great too. The success of either approach ultimately depends on you knowing what makes you tick, knowing your audience, and being consistent with your message.

You, the Shopkeeper, are the visionary behind it all. You can still step out in front as desired or needed. The key is to know why you're doing it or not and take inventory for the best use of your time and energy. Intention always matters. Identify the goals and boundaries for your marketing, disseminate the plan, and assign tasks to your team early and consistently. This will help you direct your sales flow with more ease. Marketing is effortless when it is genuine, and when you lead with your heartset, sharing information is a joy.

Key Takeaways
→ Share what excites you. The sales will follow.
→ Create trust in your team so they can share what excites them, too.
→ You can put your marketing eggs into multiple baskets, but don't forget to analyze and reflect on ROIs—from sales to your personal energy input and output.

Take Inventory
→ Why did you choose to bring a product, brand, or category into your store? What excites you about it and why?
→ How does putting yourself out there make you feel? How might you work this to your advantage?
→ What have you observed about yourself and your energy in creating and sharing through different formats?

GET NOTICED

You want to share what you're doing and what you have to offer with more people. You do all the marketing you can within the micro-ecosystem of your store, but to be amplified and supported within the commercial + community ecosystem, you must be talked about. You want and need publicity.

It's been my experience that small independent retailers receive media coverage on three occasions:

1. The business is in danger due to external market or economic factors.
2. The Shopkeeper paid for the placement.
3. It's the Christmas holiday shopping season.

In Raleigh, as in many other cities, the local media loves beer, cocktails, brunch, and anything you can hashtag with #foodiesofinstagram. It was frustrating to see how food and beverage businesses were readily and consistently revered as local brick-and-mortar destinations to know about, while retail stores were mostly left in the periphery.

Around the time PofR opened, a few longstanding local stores were relocating outside of downtown or closing altogether due to new developments. The retail talk of the town was this:

Small independent retailers were being kicked out, all small retail businesses were in danger, and Downtown Raleigh was an inhospitable, oppressive place for independent stores. The headlines were all negative, especially as portrayed by local print and TV media. While their stories might have been true, they weren't the only stories on the block. Half a dozen new independent retail stores, including mine, had opened within a few months of each other amidst the ongoing pessimistic media coverage. Fed up and frustrated with the negativity and one-sidedness—we had just invested a ton of time, energy, and money into joining the ecosystem—my husband emailed a local news anchor and kindly offered a counter story, relaying all the above.

The news anchor took the bait. A few days later, she and her cameraman visited our store, as well as a few other new retailers' stores, filming what turned out to be a spirited, upbeat, celebratory showcase of the optimistic investments and risks that were being taken in the community. We got noticed for something positive. I was thankful for my husband's proactiveness and the news anchor's interest in sharing our story.

I believe sharing, expanding, and promoting should be done because it feels right and aligns with the ecosystem in which you want to exist. I was thrilled when a local and well-respected magazine featured the store just a few months after opening our doors. The recognition was a gift for a budget-strapped business owner trying to get the word out through Instagram and word of mouth. The magazine's interest in our story was a great example of sharing, expanding, and promoting in alignment with their subscriber community.

Over the years, other local publications sought PofR and my

retail peers as "advertising partners." Rarely, if ever, were they interested in writing featured articles about our community's local retailers or putting small independent retail stores front and center on the cover—that focus remained squarely on food and drinks. But they were more than happy to take advertising dollars. Alongside nonpaid features about where to find the best brunch spot, french fries, and new beer in town were paid product placement and shopping-related features. In these magazines, the featured products and retailers were also the ones whose ads you'd find in that same issue.

Pay-to-play publications strike me as uninspired, unoriginal, and lacking interest in genuinely promoting their audience's communities. There's less to research if you only talk about the businesses that pay up. To be fair, I'm generalizing, but it does seem to be the status quo for many small local media outlets in the commercial + community ecosystem.

Unless, of course, it's the holiday season. *The Most Wonderful Time of the Year* ushers in talk about small and local shopping at no cost to the retailer. And it translates to sales! It's the time of year most Shopkeepers live for, and small independent retailers will take any love they can get, but it would be even better and more impactful if that love was felt year-round. Again, why Amex's Shop Small Movement is so great.

Food and beverage businesses get most of the love because people need to eat every day, multiple times per day. I also understand that service-based businesses are different—people need haircuts, dry-cleaning, and dental work. But from a streetscape vibrancy and community contribution standpoint, small specialty retailers are often overlooked and taken for granted.

You and your efforts deserve more recognition and

appreciation, dear Shopkeeper. Connect with the people and organizations who are happy to share what you do with their audience, and learn to spot the ones that may require a different game plan.

Key Takeaway
→ Media and print publications should want to write about your store for free because sharing, expanding, and promoting it aligns with their subscriber community.

Take Inventory
→ What story, perspective, or unique offering can you share with local media?
→ How and where are you currently telling your story and capturing people's (i.e., potential editors') attention? For example, PofR got a major national digital feature because one of the editors lived in Raleigh and followed us on Instagram.
→ If telling your story or reaching out to local media feels difficult or impossible to do, why might that be?

PAY TO GET NOTICED

I've shared my two cents on pay-to-play promotions, but intentionally paying for advertising can be a different ball game. It's possible that, after some time has passed and you've identified your audience, and whom you'd like to reach, a highly targeted approach with one or two key print publications in your area could make a significant positive impact.

Paying for ad space in magazines can seem like a big investment. However, when I reflect on how many people learned about my store too late, and how many never learned about us because I never put the store in front of them (i.e., through magazines or mailers that went straight to their house or a favorite doctor's office), perhaps the financial investment could have been worthwhile.

Press is wonderful and free (it should be free), but it's also somewhat out of your control unless you've hired a publicist. Paying for placement puts you in the driver's seat. Yes, it's a sort of A/B testing with real money, but it's an option for showing your current and future customers that you are a part of the community. In the way social media posts remind your followers of what you offer, advertisements can be visual reminders for readers to plan to visit and shop with you before or after eating "the best brunch" in town.

I briefly sold ad space in our school's newspaper during my senior year of college. My sister had done it four years prior and made good money. It seemed easy enough, and easy was precisely what I set up my senior year to be. One of the first things that I learned on the job was that it takes an average of seven times, or seven placements, for an ad to get noticed. Even then, the number can become a moving target depending on your market, the time of year, and the saturation of other advertisements. My job was to make potential ad buyers understand that once or twice wasn't enough, especially for distracted college students. Repetition was key for conversion.

Had I taken a deeper personal inventory check on my past experiences with advertising, I would have remembered all of this and tested and invested in the above. Sometimes I'd consider spending the money, but I couldn't stomach the necessary investment to achieve the repetition needed to make an impact. Additionally, my frustration with publications seeking the store as "advertising partners" instead of simply writing about us and the community's small local retailers made me want to boycott them. I didn't want to give them a dime.

My ego didn't let me see that it was a business play on all sides. They have a business to run and an audience to pander to, and my business could have used their broad local reach to increase awareness, visitors, and sales. In addition to lifestyle magazines, this kept me from seeing the value in advertising with the tourism board's visitor guide and complementary hotel maps. Whenever I saw my peers advertising with these tourism players, I'd think, *Good for them*, and wonder how I'd afford it, even though I never asked how much it cost.

You want to capture the attention of people who don't walk or drive past your store or spend time on your social media. So drop the ego, leave any money blocks behind, and consider investing in advertisements within your local community. As well as you may know your core community, you might be surprised at the new people you reach and how keen they are to exchange value with you.

Key Takeaways
- A highly targeted approach to advertising placements could be worthwhile.
- Advertisements can be visual reminders for readers to plan to visit and shop with you.

Take Inventory
- Have you been open or dismissive to paying for advertising? Why?
- What does it look and feel like to create space for paid advertisements in your monthly, quarterly, and annual budgets?
- How could paying to get noticed put you in the driver's seat for reaching more of your people? If you're already paying for advertisements, how are you evaluating the results?

BE COOL AND COLLABORATE

Collaboration is a surefire way to expand the audiences for all involved. It's also fun to cross-pollinate with players in your commercial + community ecosystem.

In the early years, when the store's walls were relatively bare, I offered them to local creatives to showcase and sell their work for a few months at a time. I curated art from painters, illustrators, graphic designers, and even from aspiring shoe designers attending the local university. Receptions were held on First Fridays, and their friends and family would come to support them. For some artists it was their first ever showcase, and it felt great to offer them the time and space. The cherry on top was that our store's walls got to tell different stories throughout the seasons.

Over time, I realized that my walls were prime real estate, and we needed to use them to display more merchandise. The artwork sold okay, but the after-hours time required to set up and break down each showcase took its toll on me month after month and further decreased any retail value they could offer. I still wanted to incorporate local art but needed a different approach. I needed to stretch out the showcase periods, change the type of art medium, and find a new location in the store.

I got my solution when I said YES to an artist's proposal for displaying her pieces as a window installation to boost her art portfolio. Her floral sculptures fit the upcoming spring season so well that it paved the way for working with local artists off the walls, which were now covered in shelves and product and into the window. Shortly after, we moved three large modular display cabinets into the window area. These cabinets offered blank canvases on the back, which were street-facing and perfect for featuring art. Every season thereafter, I worked with a different artist whose work would capture the spirit of the season in a PofR way. I paid them for the use and creation of the art, plus covered the cost of printing and materials. The result was engaging custom seasonal window art with local roots and a way to celebrate artists who also happened to be our core customers.

Remember the part about creating my own products? I would be doing myself a disservice if I didn't mention the city postcards that I created in collaboration with two local graphic designers and core customers. The postcards were intended to be cool graphic representations of the city of Raleigh and the Downtown district. In our opinion, the existing cards in the market were lame, so we joined forces to create a keepsake-worthy product that aligned with our respective businesses. I traded store credit and Instagram promotions for their work, and I paid for printing the postcards. The collaboration felt effortless, and the postcards were beloved by those who bought them. A few people even expressed that they were to be framed and hung in their home!

We also hosted lots of events. Our events ran the gamut from gatherings for a local modern architecture enthusiasts' group to playdates with the NC-based kids play sofa company, Nugget.

When we could make the space, you'd find pop-ups from local businesses, such as an ice cream shop, florist, and local makers and designers. From time to time, the store even functioned as a meeting place in the evenings for a few networking groups. Working with artists, brands, local businesses, groups, designers, and makers was a win-win, and a treat for our audiences.

Key Takeaway
→ Collaborating with players in your commercial + community ecosystem can expand the audience and be fun for all involved.

Take Inventory
→ What does collaboration mean to you?
→ What collaborations could you weave into your store's ethos, story, and mission? And with whom?
→ How can your retail space become bigger than retail?

EXPRESS YOUR GRATITUDE

Another way to treat your customers? Anniversary parties. Throwing a party for your community is a sure way to celebrate them and express your gratitude for their support. Most years we did simple things like invite people for cupcakes and champagne at the store during store hours and say a few words on Instagram. But for our third anniversary—my third magical year as a Shopkeeper—I was feeling extra good about the store and myself, and extra grateful for our community. A proper fiesta was in order.

I booked my favorite local DJ, the same one we used for our opening night, and catering from a local cafe owned by friends and shop patrons. We also worked with a local artist (who also did our window art twice) to create a custom photo booth and invited our top customers, supporters, and friends. I wanted to thank them, treat them, and host them with a special evening in the store as if they were in my home. Those three hours together, without any pretense but to enjoy each other's company in a place that brought most of us together, were so special.

There are many ways to say *thank you* and *you're appreciated*. Beyond loyalty points, rewards, and perks (like birthday discounts), expressing gratitude for your customers and community can happen through storytelling. For example, I did a short series of home visits called "PofR Visits" to celebrate some of our customers who had pieces from PofR in their homes. Imagine a Q&A feature in *Dwell* magazine, only with amateur photos that I took. Each customer had their own unique style and approach to living, and it was fun to see how they enjoyed the pieces they purchased from the store. The home visits were shared on our website, in newsletters, and through Instagram posts. They were enthusiastically received by our audience. Some customers even volunteered their own homes for future posts—they wanted in! The biggest reward of all was when our featured customers expressed how thankful they were to have those moments at home captured in time.

An aside:

I don't like to say "I should have," but I should have found a way to keep the series going. Perhaps starting it in the fall before the holiday season was madness in the making. It was just me going to my customers' homes on weekend mornings to take photos, then editing the photos and the Q&A sections in the evenings. Coming into December, I got overwhelmed by the thought of continuing to fill up my weekend mornings with home visits. I lost momentum and let PofR Visits disappear. But in its short lifespan, PofR Visits turned into a proper marketing vehicle. How could I have kept it going? I could have asked and paid for help. I had been getting to know freelance photographers through the store, and I remember thinking that one in particular might be fun to work with and was keen to take on the photography. I briefly brought it up once in conversation and she was interested, but I never followed up. It's possible that I didn't want to fully ask and pay for help. Also possible is that I perceived lack of time and energy as getting in the way of nurturing and expanding something great with someone else, for everyone else.

Gratitude can also be expressed through everyday gestures. When we stepped out from behind the cash-wrap area to personally place a shopping bag in our customers hand, we said, "Thank you," literally and physically. I learned this during my time at Nordstrom and loved the simple concluding moment of connection and appreciation. The times that we didn't do this, when we handed the bag to the customer over the cash wrap counter instead of walking out and around to them, felt off and impersonal. To rebound, I would often say an extra hearty, "Thank you! Have a nice day!" as they left the store.

If I were to do it all over again, I'd design the cash wrap counter as a floating island on the sales floor. When I shop at stores that do, this there's an instant lift in experience. Everything feels more approachable when there's not a physical barrier between people. And isn't removing barriers one of the benefits of expressing gratitude? When we show appreciation, we can create a deeper connection. And by expressing gratitude in big and small ways, the space between Shopkeeper and customer becomes less transactional and more human. It's in this space that we can recognize our respective roles in the commercial + community ecosystem and be thankful for each other in that moment.

Key Takeaways

→ There are many ways to say *thank you* and *you're appreciated* to your customers.

→ Gratitude can also be expressed through the everyday gestures you build into your way of doing business.

Take Inventory

→ What is your relationship with your customers? How would you like it to be?

→ How might you bring them into the store's experience beyond purchasing goods from you?

→ What barriers, big or small, tangible or intangible, can you remove for a greater connection with your core customers?

CONSIDER THE CONSCIOUS CUSTOMER

We had incredible customers. They were kind, enthusiastic, respectful, generous, and appreciative. But as any Shopkeeper knows, not all customers are equal. Some are more in tune with the commercial + community ecosystem than others. Some are courteous, more self-aware, and aware of the world around them. They are *conscious customers*.

For our purposes, I prefer to use the word customer over consumer, it's far more personal and truer to how we talk about the people who choose to buy from a small shop.

The definition of a *conscious customer* can expand beyond environmental, social, and fair-trade considerations. Zooming out, conscious consumption can include the understanding, or at the very least a consideration, of supply chains, micro and macro cost benefits, and conscious energy exchanges within the retail ecosystem. Understanding or considering what it takes to operate an independent retail store and the value proposition of having these stores not just exist but thrive in our communities is an important part of consumption and community making.

But as you may find, your customers might not all or always come to you with this perspective.

Customers might not consider the fact that every item they see on physical shelves has already been paid for. Even if that item sits there on consignment, a financial investment was made by someone so that they, the customer, could have the benefit and convenience of seeing it, touching it, and taking it home right then and there. It's just one of many costs alongside rent and the less obvious, but necessary, transportation for materials.

In contrast, online stores and marketplaces that are drop-ship-based don't carry similar investment costs and liabilities. They don't pay for or carry inventory up front or at the time of a customer's purchase. They simply place an order with the product vendor once the sale is made and money from the customer is received. The only product investment made on the retailer's part is the time spent adding the product to their website and coordinating the final order if it's not done automatically.

Drop-ship programs can be wonderful, I used them for my store as much as possible. But brick-and-mortar stores, unless specifically set up as showrooms as many large direct-to-consumer (DTC) companies have done, can rarely operate exclusively on a drop-ship model. They must first spend money to make money. Small independent retail stores are typically not showrooms or brand experiences, though a few new concepts are challenging this in larger markets. For now, however, mom-and-pop shops remain predominantly if not exclusively inventory-based businesses.

Practices like visiting a store to see a product in person but then searching for it online to buy at a cheaper price, called showrooming, can really hurt small merchants. Even buying something once from a small merchant but then seeking to repurchase the same item online can hurt the bottom line. I'll never forget the time a customer visited, months after purchasing incense sticks from us. She was raving about how much she loved them, had been out of them for a while, and was desperate to buy more. She went on to tell me that she searched and searched and searched *all over the internet* for them but came up empty-handed for where to buy them. So she, "*had* to come back to the store!" There was a reason for that. I sourced those incense sticks directly from Japan, and I was the only US retailer selling them. They were obscure at the time, and their uniqueness was precisely the benefit that my store brought to the market and to her.

So there she was, standing right in front of the incense sticks, right where she had discovered them, *literally in the place she could buy them again*. But instead of valuing that I had spent the energy to stock them in my store for her to discover, and financially invested in that discovery, she chose to spend her own energy and time searching elsewhere (for a cheaper price maybe?). She lived without a resupply for weeks when she could have just bought them from us and enjoyed them all along. She lived nearby, so proximity to the store couldn't have been the issue. But if leaving her house was indeed a problem, she could have shopped on our online store, and we would have shipped or hand-delivered them to her. We did curbside pickups upon request and local deliveries before the pandemic made it a norm. It seemed like this customer went out of her way to not shop with us again.

In the expanded definition of a conscious customer, I saw this as a massive fail. She wasted personal time and energy, not recognizing opportunity costs and benefits, and was disconnected to the value that the store offered her within the commercial +

community ecosystem. This simple act, done repeatedly by many consumers over time, can greatly affect cash flow for independent merchants. Without a healthy cash flow, there is no long-term business.

As a shopper myself, if a store speaks to me somehow, I try to buy something right then and there, even if it's just a cool store-branded pencil. I know that I don't owe them anything but it's my way of saying *thank you for existing*. Thank you for inspiring me. I'm even more invested if the store was a destination and my experience met or exceeded expectations. I liken it to planning or going to a restaurant, coffee shop, or bar. If I make an extra effort to experience that restaurant, coffee shop, or bar, would I ever show up, let myself be seated, and leave without making a purchase? Nope. I would at least order a drink. Different industries and behaviors, of course, but the exchange of energies, mental and monetary, are more alike than not.

PofR became a destination, but if you wanted to come by on a Monday or Tuesday, you needed to make an appointment. I chose to close two days a week so that I could (mostly) get one day off and one day to work on store projects and tasks that were easier to do while closed to the public. Few people ever took us up on making appointments. Comments like, "No, I don't need to bother you on your day off. I'll make another day work," were always appreciated. Such comments were a sign of a conscious customer, even if, at times, it pained me to know that our hours weren't convenient for everyone. The appointments made and kept were by intentional shoppers, meaning, they knew exactly what they wanted to look at and buy, a form of conscious consumption.

One day, I accepted a Monday appointment for someone who had friends in town; it was the only day they had available, and she *really* wanted to show them the store. I already had plans with my family but made it work since she seemed so excited, and perhaps that excitement would lead to a decent enough sale to make the time on my day off worth it.

It was a late-morning appointment, and I arrived thirty minutes before to set up the iPad and cashbox, turn on the A/C and lights, and do some quick dusting and tidying up. She and her group arrived as scheduled. They looked like they were just out of college, and I'll admit my immediate disappointment. While they seemed to love our store, the college and just-out-of-college demographic were not typically our biggest spenders. Yet I gave them the benefit of the doubt and welcomed them in with a big smile. They were friendly, we chatted briefly, and a whole three minutes later they were gone. The woman who had made the appointment meant that she wanted to literally "show them the store." There was no intent to purchase anything. It's also possible that the store didn't meet their expectations, and they decided then and there that there was nothing worth buying. Either way, I was stunned and then mad; appointments had never gone that way before. My time didn't seem to matter to them, but it mattered to me.

Shortly after that, I watched a movie on Netflix called *The Unicorn Store*, featuring Samuel L. Jackson as the Shopkeeper, if you can call him that in the wonderfully strange film. In one scene, the protagonist, a young woman who wants nothing more in life than to have a unicorn, and this store had the promise of making that dream come true, makes a comment that doesn't go over well with the frustrated Shopkeeper. The exchange goes like this:

— (Shopkeeper) *Has anyone ever told you that you are a very selfish person?*
— *Huh?*
— *You think everything in this store is for you?!*
— *Well, you kind of said it was . . .*
— *You think a store is only customers, or did it ever occur to you that maybe, just maybe, the salespeople on the other side have their own lives, their own dreams, their own reason for selling the things they sell? Geez Louise!*

I laughed so hard. I saw myself in Samuel L. Jackson's character. His response to his customer was how I felt after the appointment, and in so many other moments at the store as a Shopkeeper, salesperson, human being. Had I had the balls, I would have created a meme out the performance to post on our store's Instagram because sometimes I just needed to vent about certain encounters. It was such a great scene to experience through a Shopkeeper's lens.[ii]

Another very specific occurrence and example of a not-so-conscious customer happened to my team while I was away, and thankfully only happened once. This customer had declared with exuberance that the stepladder she found with us was just what she needed. It was the *coolest stepladder* she'd ever seen. I was so happy to meet her need in this way. Unfortunately, she returned to the store a few days later to ask if she could return the ladder unless we could match Amazon's price and get store credit for $50, as that's how much less Amazon was selling it for. Wow.

Not only did she spend extra time and energy searching for a better deal, even though she had been satisfied with her purchase, she seemed completely unaware of, or chose to disregard, the possible reasons for a price difference between Amazon and a small retailer like ours. Reasons that start from the makers and distributor and filter down to smaller players that can't compete with Amazon's economies of scale. And weren't trying to. If she wanted the $50 back in her bank account, we would have graciously accepted a return and processed the refund. My team, and then I, couldn't believe the request to match Amazon, especially since we had just reopened the store during the pandemic. And for the record, we were carrying the *coolest step ladder* long before it was available on the online megastore.

Having said all of this, I recognize that people shop for different reasons. And that my store, and the things inside of it, served different purposes for everyone.

From the joys and celebrations that brought customers in to make a purchase, to the heavy stresses of life that called for a form of design and retail therapy, I learned a lot about our customers over five years. The store was there for them, and in many cases, so was our team. PofR served as a visual and emotional refuge for some and as a visual energetic source of inspiration for others. You will come to see this and more in your store; it can be a beauty to witness and participate in.

People bring different energies and intentions into their purchasing journey. That's why it's critical to know yourself as a Shopkeeper so you can manage your emotions, expectations, and responses to the less-delightful situations like the ones shared above. If you're not in a good place, they can easily turn you sour for longer than necessary and harm your customer and employee interactions. You will learn to take a deep breath and give these customers grace; you don't know what's happening in their world. And on the flip side, you may not be the customer you think you are or would be.

Key Takeaways
- → *Conscious customers* are courteous, are aware of the world around them, are knowledgable about their own opportunity costs and benefits, and are in tune with the commercial + community ecosystem.

Take Inventory
- → What are your expectations for people's behaviors, experiences, and responses inside and about your store?
- → How can observation and compassion come forth in less desirable customer interactions instead of reaction and judgment?
- → If people bring different energies and intentions into their store visit, how can you best prepare to serve and meet them where they're at?

GOOD INTENTIONS

The sad truth is that I've become one of *them*. Not them as in the customers described in the above section, but another kind of shopper I also got to know well. I've caught myself saying and thinking their familiar line, "I rarely make it out here, or out there." This and similar phrases were often said by people who loved the store from afar through Instagram and our website, and years later *finally* made it to the store in person. They lived far away, were generally preoccupied, or too busy. It was also said by people who expressed their desire to come in more often but *life, kids, work* all made it hard to do.

Part of me would sympathize, but another would think *bullshit*. Especially if they lived within a fifteen-minute radius of the store. I felt like everyone else, particularly those with nine-to-five jobs, had all the time in the world and that any reason not to come to the store, when they *really* wanted to, was an excuse. They had weekends. People without kids had evenings. People who were freelancers could make their own schedules and surely swing by the store whenever they wanted to. And people with kids could bring their kids. We loved kids! No excuses. Or so I thought.

No longer living Shopkeeper hours, I can relate and truly appreciate the desire to want to visit a store, a restaurant, or a coffee shop for the first time or more frequently, but not actually do it. I have kids who are all-consuming in beautiful and very demanding ways. I have work, personal tasks, and desires that are also consuming in beautiful and demanding ways. At home there are things to be cleaned and cooked, kids to be with. Outside of the home, there are errands to run. Parks to take the kids to. Nature walks to take. My "free" time rarely includes leisurely walking around town or a shopping center just popping in and out of places. Unless I'm on vacation. Then walking around and popping in and out of shops is *all* I want to do, and it's prioritized. Forget history tours and sightseeing trollies; point me to the nearest independent shops to get a sense of the local flavor.

Now I better appreciate how day-to-day life can take over. Even the best intentions to pop into a store can change when there's no easy parking.

When I visit new stores or stores I've come to love, there is usually a mission. I'm either shopping for something specific that we want or need for our home and ourselves, a gift, or a service. This outing is either put on my actions list or added to the calendar if it's a particularly packed day with time requirements. I've also likely confirmed that they have what I want or need by checking out their website or Instagram. It's not how I prefer my #shopsmall shopping to go, a leisurely sense of in-person discovery is way more satisfying, but it's usually the way that it plays out these days if I'm not on holiday. And when I *really* want to shop in person, browse, and focus? I go without my kids.

So yes, now I get it. It's not bullshit; it is life. Yet when I catch myself saying or thinking, "I rarely make it here or out there," and delay a visit for something I know I'll eventually buy anyway, I feel a bit guilty and hypocritical. I recognize that there's a business and a Shopkeeper behind it with overhead to pay who could use my business today versus in two or ten months from now. I know an ecosystem is involved, and having been on the other side of the cash wrap counter, I want to be a conscious player as a customer and community member.

Key Takeaways
→ Good intentions from your customers really are good. Have empathy and gratitude for them.

Take Inventory
→ Do you question, criticize, or become cynical about your customer's behaviors? What might this be reflecting about yourself in those moments?
→ What personal needs are not being met if and when you find yourself thinking the above?
→ How can you flip the script and focus on staying connected with your customers between visits so that it's a joy for them to "finally" make it? And for you to serve them?

PART VI
ONWARD

LEARNING TO TAKE PERSONAL INVENTORY

Four years into our five-year lease, I took on the belief that the store would never pay back the value that I put into it, at least financially. In time it would, but I was starting to see the end of my Shopkeeper Dream. Sure, the 40 percent and 60 percent monthly jumps in year-over-year sales were exciting and encouraging, but they weren't enough to sustain or motivate me to keep the store going.

I started looking around at my retail peers to see what might be different for them, for their journeys and successes, from the outside looking in. I sensed that for many of them, their store was a major long-term plan. It was precisely how they desired to exist in and share with the world. My store was always a big plan and a big deal, but I hadn't decided that it was what I wanted to be doing, and where I wanted to be doing it, for more than five years. My timeline had always been open to possibilities after the five-year lease term expired: renew and stay the course, change location to expand and evolve, or sell, close, and move on. That's why I pushed to pay off our loan within the same period of time. With our lease expiration around the corner, I had a decision to make.

The store's manifesto, *Experience Your Everyday*, had been at work within me, and I began to tune in to my own experiences and energies. I asked myself how I wanted to experience my everyday on an emotional level and began questioning what success meant to me at this point in life.

Little by little, I started taking new personal inventory with a heartset approach: *Was the Shopkeeper Dream ever really for me? What made me desire to have a store in the first place? What could I have done differently with how I operated the store? What am I supposed to be doing instead? Do I really want to be a full-time stay-at-home mom? Or am I longing for a better professional fit?*

The answers started coming in.

After the emotional dust from my maternity leave and Hazel's diagnosis settled, I made space for reading again. I picked up a book about highly spirited children, seeking to learn about our highly spirited four-year-old, and ended up learning more about myself. The book dove into personality types, introverts and extroverts, and the spectrum in between. I'd always assumed that these personality traits had to do with being naturally social or not. Prior to reading *Raising Your Highly Spirited Child* by Mary Sheedy Kurcinka, I would say that I leaned toward extroversion since I enjoy and am comfortable being social. Man was I wrong.

Introversion and extroversion are not about how social you are; they're about how you *get* and *spend* your energy. How you recharge your batteries and how you spend that charge. My batteries did not, and do not, get charged by being social all day. Learning this opened the floodgates for understanding why I'd spent the past four years feeling frustrated with my workflow as a shopkeeper and why I'd often come home exhausted rather than elated after a full day at the store.[iii]

I spent my shopkeeping days talking with people, strangers and friends alike, and engaging on Instagram. I was highly social for eight straight hours a day. I genuinely enjoyed most of it, but with a new understanding of introversion and extroversion, I could see how and why my day-to-day work ultimately made me feel the way I did. There were times when I wanted nothing more than to disappear into the backroom to work quietly and undisturbed. I loved the days when there were two or three of us on the schedule and I could tuck away to work *on* the business instead of *in* it. Being socially "on" for so much of the day was draining, but it took nearly four years of full-time work at the front of the house to put language and better context around those feelings.

I could have saved myself a lot of angst in that department had I taken personal inventory sooner and looked back to my fifth-grade yearbook (yes, we had a fifth-grade yearbook, and I've kept it all these years, stored in LA and dusted off in Raleigh, likely for this exact revelation). Each fifth grader was asked what we wanted to be when we grew up, and my response was, "A secretary for a big company." Odd but intriguing. I've always had an entrepreneurial spirit, so working for someone else was never my deepest desire. There was more to my response. What I wanted was a command center. An organized and dedicated space to take care of business and feel confident in my work and progress. My fifth-grade self had no intention of actually being someone's secretary, but the commandeering, get-shit-done attitude and presence that she saw in "big company" secretaries appealed to her. Her desire was still in me.

The cash wrap became my default command center. And while I could get shit done, I rarely did it through focus and flow. At the store, I was on from opening to closing with constant customers and social conversations, aka interruptions. At home, where I could technically work in the morning before I left for the store or in the evenings after I got home from work and bedtimes had passed, I was on for my kids, which were also interruptions. When you're a parent, your energy and space are rarely your own, especially if you live in a one-bedroom open-floor-plan condo like we did.

The space and time for deep work could have been created had I been more aware and proactive about the conditions needed to do my best work. For example, we had a second-floor mezzanine that we used for storage and housing the giant HVAC unit. The area was private and out of site. I could have easily moved things around to set up a comfortable workspace. On the days that I had help on the floor, I could have worked up there, uninterrupted with headphones on, instead of sitting in the crowded, and often busy, backroom telling myself, *This is less than ideal*. Resenting the lack of space and time for focused work was just one of many ways that I enjoyed torturing myself.

In addition to revisiting my fifth-grade yearbook, had I paid attention to my past satisfaction with workflow and work environments, and what lit me up, I might have recognized my requirements long before my sanity depended on it. I loved past jobs that were 80 percent head-down work at my desk and 20 percent active, out-of-office engagement. I also relished the times when I took care of our home and stayed in it to write my blog, work on client projects, and ventured out at my discretion. Very little about my retail workflow and lifestyle—my Shopkeeper Dream—fit the past work experiences that I thrived in.

To give ourselves the best chance to thrive, we must lead with our heartset. We can't ignore or dismiss our practical past work experiences, strengths, and tested skill sets as can be found on our resume; rather, we have to prioritize what is true about our truest selves. We have to consider how we felt, operated, and existed day to day within those roles. We need to qualify the aspects of our personal experiences that are hard, and perhaps impossible, to relay on a traditional CV. Had I launched my store with the above reflections and insights, I'm certain that I could have felt, operated, and existed better as a shopkeeper—and mom, partner, and human.

The holidays were fast approaching, and by this point, I was certain that I wanted to move on from the store. I didn't want to permanently close PofR; I wanted to sell the brick-and-mortar and online store so that both could stay in the community and continue for the customers who loved PofR. I also wanted a chance to recuperate our financial investment. A lot of factors played into my decision, but the overarching theme was that owning and operating a store was no longer for me.

Years prior, in a bio for my personal website, I wrote, "I'm happiest when creating." Flash-forward to my present Shopkeeping days, I was creating less and managing more with no end in sight. I could feel my spark dwindling, but this time it wasn't burnout . . . I was boring out. It was me at TOMS, swimming in RFPs and spreadsheets, dying to feel creative all over again. I couldn't change my job like I did back then, but I could expand what I did through the job I had created. I could work on a related side project that made my heart sing beyond the store's physical limits, marketing budget, and daily tasks. I knew that I had one more year left as a Shopkeeper, and knowing this felt liberating.

With a renewed sense of purpose, I penned a plan to bring together a group of talented emerging furniture and textile designers from the area. I had gotten to know them through the store and knew they struggled to find a proper space to display their talents. They deserved a dedicated space and time for the public to engage with their creations, so I put together an event that would do just that. I was also painfully aware that I had yet to solidify the export element of my original vision of the store. We called the event *New Carolina*, a two-day showcase of contemporary design from North Carolina makers. It was a proof-of-concept. If successful, the event would expand to host more designers and categories down the road.

After a two-month whirlwind of event design, coordination, team efforts, and securing sponsorship from a major North Carolina-based furniture manufacturer, New Carolina took place in early February 2020. The event was a hit, and the concept was officially proven. It was fun and meaningful for all involved and lit me up. New Carolina made me feel like me again—bringing a vision to life, people and things together, and making magic happen for all to experience. It got me back into a flow of creativity and deepened my desire for more creative expressions, retail-related or not. I got my spark back.

In letting go of the store, I fell back in love with it. I was eager to have fun during our final dance, even though I knew that a lot of footwork was still ahead. And with the workload, I would not burn out or descend into my own madness. Instead, when the now-familiar roller coaster of negative emotions arose, a world of helpful questions and considerations would open up in my mind. The practice of taking personal inventory would prove essential in the months to come.

The pandemic started shortly thereafter, changing many things for me, as it did for everyone else. The New Carolina proof-of-concept was put on the back burner, and I became absorbed in the uncertainties of the shutdowns and the constant pivoting required for my final year of business. The biggest of them all—selling PofR was no longer an option. The store owners and property developers I planned to reach out to early that spring were now consumed with their own uncertainties. It was a good thing that I had spent the year prior processing the idea of moving on from the store, otherwise 2020 could have rocked me even more. I had already mentally checked out of the store. Not in an abandonment sense, but in a way that gave me comfort, knowing I could keep operating it with new expectations, a positive heartset approach, and a productive mindset.

Still, this was a different ending than planned. This was now the very final year of PofR. Period.

The irony of closing a home goods store mid-pandemic, when the entire world woke up to the value of the objects and experiences in their homes, was not lost on me. I fought my ego with every newly published article that spoke to the importance of having things you love in your home as if the approach was a new revelation. All the same, I was thankful for them because from a business perspective, selling home goods during that time had serious advantages. We didn't sell essential items like food or toilet paper, but enough people were sick of staring at and using things they didn't love. We were there to help fulfill their wants and needs; in return, we got to keep our cash flow and operations afloat pretty well, all things considered. Our online store served as a lifeline for serving our customers and helping us stay afloat; thank goodness I had spent the past several years making it a digital copy of the brick-and-mortar store, whereas some of my retail peers were scrambling to get started.

The emotional and financial support from our local community and newly acquired online customers from across the country was everything I could have hoped for PofR's final year. The interest and media push for home goods and simple indulgences like puzzles and unscented candles was comforting and validating that what we offered, objects that help people experience their everyday for the better, did matter. People who knew of my plan to close would ask if I was going to keep the online store going, but that was not in the cards. I no longer wanted to have a physical place of business with physical products to manage, and an online store is not unlike a brick-and-mortar store in that sense. I was ready to move on completely and explore my energetic sparks once more.

You know the saying, "You don't know what you have until it's gone"?

Well, you also don't know what you've offered until you take it away.

After the closing announcement, I received public and private messages on social media and email that went straight to my heart. Some people even hand-delivered and snail-mailed thank-you cards. I couldn't believe it. Thank you cards? I felt grateful and terrible at the same time. I knew that we had created something that people enjoyed, but to receive thank-you cards, as if I did something really nice for them? Their personal notes shared what the store had come to mean to them and expressed sadness over how much it would be missed. They all wished me well in my next chapter. Being the bearer and creator of bad news was tough, and the response from our community took me by surprise. A few people even expressed that they felt like they'd been punched in the gut. Granted, this all occurred mid-pandemic, so bad news and disappointments were weighing on everyone. For that reason, people's thoughtful gestures and kind words felt extraordinary, and they brought me back to a major reason for starting the store: *to offer something of value*.

Six months later, I ran into a friend and super-supporter of the store who I hadn't seen since closing. Within thirty seconds he expressed how much the store positively impacted the community and his current work. I couldn't believe the generosity coming out of his mouth, but I was ready to receive it without feeling terrible for having taken it away. A part of me was glad that I didn't know the depth of the store's impact as he saw it. The depth of my impact as he expressed it. Creating and operating the store in the way that I did at any given moment was what I knew to do, even when I struggled through it sometimes. The nice things people said about their experiences with PofR, both in store and online, were gifts letting me know that the store indeed created value for many people and was lasting beyond its existence.

portofraleigh

The time has come to say thank you and goodbye.

After nearly five years of business, PofR will be closing our storefront and online operations on August 23. Your support, enthusiasm, and patronage made this dream-store possible, and we are eternally grateful. We would not have stayed in business this long without you!

I made the decision last year to prioritize family. With our lease ending this fall and Covid-19 upon us, the time is now. I became mom to our first daughter at the same time PofR was born. The first few years felt like a never ending roller coaster ride as I learned to simultaneously navigate and nurture two new worlds. We now have a second daughter and with my feet firmly on the ground, I'm excited to pursue new opportunities with family and career.

I've learned so much about the ins-and-outs of building, owning, and operating every detail of a retail store, and I'm proud of what we've accomplished. I speak on behalf of our team in saying that we will miss our in-store moments, connections, and conversations. We are so lucky to have witnessed your own evolutions from graduations to new jobs, from engagements to growing families.

Our online friends: thank you for choosing to shop with us in a sea of endless options. I hope that we got a chance to see you in our brick and mortar at least once during a visit to Raleigh.

Thank you for giving us the opportunity to create, play, and grow in this bright space with you.

I wanted so badly to have a big closing/thank you party with hugs all around, but we'll have to make the best of these strange times. Stay tuned here as we look back at all of the fun we've had at 416 S. McDowell St. and of course, tomorrow for info on our closing sale that begins August 1(!).

It has been an honor and a pleasure. Thank you, thank you, thank you!!!

JULY 27, 2020

Add a comment...

Key Takeaways
- → To give yourself the best chance to thrive, you must lead with your heartset. Re-discover it by taking personal inventory.
- → Reflect and consider how you felt, operated, and existed within your past resume's roles, day to day, and apply it to your present.

Take Inventory
- → How do you want to experience your every day on an emotional level at this stage of your Shopkeeper Journey? How is that similar or different from when you started? Your past roles that led you here?
- → What has felt supportive and expansive in your day-to-day operations as a Shopkeeper, and what has not?
- → Where might there be opportunities to create the support, time and space, or creative fuel you need, using what's available to you now?

REFRAMING THE JOURNEY

Whether you run your business for five decades or five months, the people who come in and out of your shop will leave an imprint on your life. Some become friends, some bring fleeting yet beautiful moments of connection, and some unintentionally teach you about yourself and human nature, for better or for worse.

Next to your personal energy and way of being, the people who come in and out of your store are the most important members of your commercial + community ecosystem. Recognize, nurture, and honor the good ones, and brush off the rest. Enjoy the moments you create together, with as much awareness and presence as possible.

Even though the Shopkeeper Dream I chose to chase was completely counter to the lifestyle I ultimately wanted, it was a container that nurtured more than my personal passions and skill sets. The beautiful ball and chain that was PofR paved a path to something that I deeply longed for: a sense of community.

In the process of closing the store, I would often think, *I can't wait to finally live in Raleigh*. For five years, I felt like I'd lived within the two-block radius between the store and our condo.

Of course, this is a gross exaggeration but, compared to the way I truly wanted to experience the city, state, and people who I'd come to know and love, I felt boxed-in. I wanted to have more time and energy to go on dinner and coffee dates with friends and to do fun things with my family and our friends' families. I, too, wanted to check out the *"Best brunch spots in town!"*

It turns out, I didn't need to do those things to experience *living* in my city. Being at the store, a place where shared interests and passions came together, connecting with people daily and playing and growing in it with my family, *that* was me experiencing where I lived. I didn't have to go all over town or the state to be with my community because the store, right where I stood, *was my community*. Without my Shopkeeper Dream, I might have never met the people I did and experienced the things I did—inside and outside of its four walls.

Recognizing this was a valuable reframing and reminder not to worry about the life we may think we're not living. Sometimes what we desire might be right in front of our nose; it just looks different than we imagined. Whether that desire is to experience your community like me, or other aspects of your Shopkeeper Dream, it pays dividends to reflect on and reframe what might actually be true.

Key Takeaway
→ The desires you have for your Shopkeeper life are authentic and valid. But the way they manifest may be different than you originally imagined. Reflect to reframe.

Take Inventory
→ What were your desires and values when you started? How have they evolved during the lifespan of your store?
→ What do you often think or complain about that could be reframed to see what's in your world now but might look different than imagined?
→ Are there surprising outcomes from your Shopkeeper efforts that make your heart smile?

HOW'S THE FIT?

Some entrepreneurs find the right fit with their first business. Some with their tenth. These entrepreneurs turn their ideas, passions, and skills into a thriving and impactful business for themselves and the customers they serve. When I read or hear their stories, I often see indications that their mindset and heartset are perfectly aligned. They merged their resume's technical skills and practical experiences with their natural talents, ways of being, and their heart's deepest desires.

Success stories from such entrepreneurs who have "made it" can inspire, motivate, and guide fellow entrepreneurs, but they can also be hard to relate to when you're on your own path and process. *What about those who didn't "make it" past year two, five, or ten for any number of reasons? What lessons and insights do they have to share, and how do they measure success?*

The journey to the right fit is different for everyone. When we learn to recognize other people's aligned heartset and mindset through different lenses and contexts—traditionally successful vs. still seeking—we can begin to recognize our own.

Being highly intentional and discerning about the items we carried at PofR taught me how to be highly intentional and discerning about everything in life. For half a decade, I danced between wanting the store to serve my needs and desires while tuning in to the needs and desires of our customers. Ultimately, that dance didn't satisfy.

I once heard philosopher and author, Eckart Tolle, share on a podcast that if something doesn't satisfy you, it's the ego. That notion made so much sense; I was not satisfied with my current fit, and my self-worth reflected it. While the store certainly created value for some people in the community, it existed because *I*, *Ana Maria Muñoz* had a Shopkeeper Dream that *I* needed to fulfill along with its related markers of success. When we moved to Raleigh, the market was not asking for my store. I just showed up to a new town and proclaimed that the community needed what I wanted to see in the world. Realizing that this entire venture was more ego-driven than I had ever imagined was humbling, to say the least.[iv]

We all need a bit of ego to accomplish things in life, but it's safe to say that not all Shopkeepers are alike in their subconscious and conscious intentions. I'm in awe of the ones who have aligned their heartset and mindset to find their right fit. This can be seen in the Shopkeepers who run their stores out of passion but also as a disciplined business. They've been doing it for five years, ten years, or longer, and their stores are beautiful reflections of themselves with teams who carry out the vision daily. These Shopkeepers share what they want to see in the world through small, independent retail. They do it all well enough that customers keep returning. Some Shopkeepers even make a solid living out of it.

I've thought a lot about what kind of personality, desire, or stage of life is required for a long-term and fulfilling role as an independent Shopkeeper. One example of stage of life meeting a passion always stands out to me. A local news outlet shared the story of a longstanding bookstore owner who doesn't work for profit but out of love. The owner and Shopkeeper started the business after retiring from a career in the private and public sectors in the field of radiation: "On the first nuclear-powered submarine . . . on X-rays, microwave ovens, things like that." He even worked on the Manhattan Project. But his true love was books. He retired in 1977, set up shop, and, thanks to a government pension, has never taken a salary from the store. Not only does he not take a salary after forty years of Shopkeeping, he also supports employees and donates a large percentage of sales revenue every year to local organizations.[v]

This booklover found a way to share his passion with his community during a stage of life that, perhaps, made it easier to share. Prior to shopkeeping, he completed chapters in his career that might have stemmed from personal and intellectual curiosities and strengths. When retirement came and he had financial security for the rest of his life. Since he didn't need anything but joy from it, the decision to share his passion for books through retail made for a great fit. He'd been-there-done-that and was satisfied living his Shopkeeper Dream, stating, "There's nowhere else I'd rather be than here." That last bit, I've realized, is a crucial element to being an independent Shopkeeper for the long haul; you must want to live, work, and play exactly where your store is.

The season of life I was experiencing clashed with the lack of awareness I had about myself and my truest desires. I still wanted to travel. I wanted to live in other places again. I wanted to create more things and experiences. I wanted to be with my family more. The chapter of life I was in, and still am, is much closer to the front cover of a book than the back cover. While I didn't see myself in that bookstore Shopkeeper, I definitely understood him. The *right fit* is different for every person and will surface at different times.

Like the bookshop owner, the reason the Shopkeeper Dream dialed your number could be that it is your calling, or *right fit*, right now. You've picked up the phone call and plan to stay on the line for a long, *long* time. Or ultimately, you're like me and you've picked up the call to stay on the line for a short while; the call is great, but other calls are coming in too. You can keep listening or hang up to pick up new lines—both are equally okay.

Just like with past ventures—Ring Cozy, The Pond Market, and Anamu accessories—I followed energetic sparks, seized opportunities, adapted, and evolved from where I stood. Shopkeeping wasn't my long-term fit, but it was just the right size for the place and time. Wherever I was geographically and emotionally, each act of creation and subsequent growth created momentum for the next. This type of personal evolution is why we keep sharpening and caring for our tools as we go. We get to define our right fit and version of success. We get to adjust, grow, and move forward.

Every Shopkeeper, whether past, present, or future, will have their reasons and seasons for sharing their passions through a store. The Shopkeeper Dream can be for a single season or a lifetime; it can be a hobby or a career. I've discovered that the secret to being a successful Shopkeeper at any age and stage of life is to release a focus on profits or ego-driven outcomes. Do it because it's all that you want to do, share, and see more of in the world. It's an experience that you feel called to create for yourself and for others.

Key Takeaways
- The *right fit* for your business is when your mindset and heartset align.
- The *right fit* is different for every person and will surface at different times. We get to define our right fit and version of success.

Take Inventory
- What does this statement make you feel? What comes to mind in regards to your fit? "The secret to being a successful Shopkeeper at any age and stage of life is to release a focus on profits or ego-driven outcomes. Do it because it's all that you want to do, share, and see more of in the world. It's an experience that you feel called to create for yourself and for others."
- How can you give yourself the grace to answer the above honestly? How can you celebrate a right fit, give yourself permission to evolve it, or move on and keep looking?
- How can you honor your heartset, stay curious, and commit to taking personal inventory along the way?

WHICH ROAD WILL YOU TAKE?

Stores that stay in one location or move and evolve in different spaces within their community are like evergreen trees in nature's ecosystem. They are rooted and nurtured by their surroundings and are present for a very long time.

Other small shops are perennial. They come and go, share their flare, then disappear for another season of life to begin. The empty shopfronts perennials leave behind are seedlings full of potential ready to be rewilded through the passions, interests, and expertise of new Shopkeepers.

My store was ultimately a perennial, and I experienced my storefront's rewilding through serendipity, ego, and release.

When it came time for us to vacate our storefront, I hoped that the next tenant would not keep the faux yellow "shipping container" that we built as a backroom and design feature. It felt too specific to PofR. But the new tenant, a tattoo and art studio, kept it all down to the shelves we mounted on the walls. Part of me thought, *Smart move to not invest on any changes* (after my build-out lessons), but my ego screamed, *Pleeeeeaaaase make it your own! The yellow shipping container was my brand, my touch, my vision!*

As fate would have it, the owner and artist of the studio was our new neighbor in the condo building where I lived two blocks away. The moment I met him, my ego about the space completely faded away. He was the perfect person to take it as-is. Not only because he exuded positive energy but because he had "shipping container" at the top of his wish list. He told me that he practically did a backflip when his leasing agent showed him the space. My ending was destined to be his new beginning.

In a way, my old shop's new tenant played a role in my new beginning. I'd been thinking about a particular tattoo design for over a decade and decided that it was finally time to go for it. Who better to do it, in what better place, than in my new neighbor's new tattoo studio? I was nervous to take the plunge, but as I sat in his chair and experienced my former space transformed through his art and vision, I knew that I made the right decision many times over.

At some point you will have a decision to make: stay, evolve, or move on. Every Shopkeeper is faced with these three options at some point in their Shopkeeper journey. Perhaps your lease is up for renewal or your best-selling product categories are cause for a pivot. Maybe your services are more successful than your products or your family's needs have changed. Maybe your neighborhood has changed . . . you've changed.

It's at these crossroads that taking personal inventory is essential. By asking yourself, *Is this the right fit?* you create space for the best answer or solution to surface. This supports how you define success.

Staying

It's all working like a well-oiled machine. You've found a stride and pace in your operations that works for you, your team, and your customers. You give the people what they want, the business is profitable or confidently on its way to profitability. You feel fulfilled and purposeful. The value you've created is good as is; the reliability of what you offer your customers, and how, is as solid as the foundation you've built. You have found your right fit as a Shopkeeper. The location, the product, the services, the team you've built, and the community you serve fit perfectly together. The store serves your personal needs as a business or hobby. It all works well for you and, besides refreshing merchandise to keep your audience interested, there's very little, if anything, that needs to change at this point.

Evolving

It's all working like a well-oiled machine, but something with the business *must* change. Your landlord doesn't renew your lease, and you must find a new location. Or you *need* a new location to better serve your customers and business growth. Perhaps what people come to you for has evolved from where you started. For example, you started selling mostly books and stationery, but now people want more giftable lifestyle items, or vice versa. It's an evolution of your core offerings that affects every decision from your buying to available floorspace and marketing.

Or everything could be working like a well-oiled machine, but your personal needs have changed. You're satisfied with the store's progress, but you sense that there's something more you could be contributing to it through your specific skill sets and zone of genius. You want to stop wearing all the hats and start focusing on the parts of the business that light you up the most. Perhaps evolving has nothing to do with you, rather your family's needs have changed and will require more time and attention than the business currently allows.

It's time to act so that the business can keep going as intended. Transformations, no matter how big or small, can be tough at first. We can easily feel overwhelmed by the shifts ahead of us and all that's required to get us there. But once the need is identified, be it a new location, a change in inventory, growing and entrusting a team, or dedicating more time and energy to your family, you must trust that this need will be met, no matter what.

Moving On

The shop is doing fine to spectacular, but you're longing for something different. Maybe the Shopkeeper role and lifestyle no longer satisfy your personal, creative, and entrepreneurial desires. Maybe your family's needs have changed and there's no longer room for the business.

Or you're still madly in love with being a Shopkeeper but the shop is *not* doing great. You're struggling financially, even though you've done and tried everything to make it work. The local response isn't what you expected and hoped for. The overall resonance isn't there to make your business work in the long run. It's not looking pretty.

This pivotal crossroad is one where you decide the fate of the business. Do you stay and evolve with it? Sell it to new ownership and management? Close it altogether?

If you sell your business, fantastic. A new Shopkeeper gets to live out their dream. Your community can continue to enjoy what you started and, hopefully, your sale price and terms are more than satisfactory.

If you close, whatever the reason may be, know that you started the whole venture because you are a creative being who has something to offer this world. The Shopkeeper Dream may not have been your *right fit*, but something else surely is and will be. Consider your time with the store like a seed that's been taking root in the background, ready for it's time to be tended in a new season of life. Remember, each act of creation and subsequent growth creates momentum for the next. Know that your ending might be someone else's new beginning. The gift keeps on giving.

At the end of the day, our journey is all about creating value for other people and ourselves. We do this step by step.

Every choice we make and every experience we have creates new choices and experiences. They may not always be easy, pleasant, or desired, but we always, *always*, have the opportunity to learn and grow from them. We must remain open. We must listen to the whispers coming from deep within us, get curious, and take personal inventory often and honestly. We must take risks, say *YES*, step out of comfort zones. We must bet on ourselves so that we may serve our family, friends, and our communities. And yes, without a doubt, serve ourselves. The entrepreneurial experience is one that we must trust in and give thanks for as it unfolds.

Living the Shopkeeper Dream is a personal masterclass in learning to honor who we are at our core and giving ourselves permission to take inspired action at any stage in our lives, with or without that inner knowledge. We do all that we can with the time, energy, resources, and consciousness that we have in every moment. And we do it all with the hope that we'll be supported by externalities in the ecosystems we jump into just as much, if not more, than the internal ones we can control.

At all times we can check in with ourselves and value the present moment.

Just like a retail store's ever-changing inventory, we, too, are ever-changing. Just like a retail store's inventory, we, too, require frequent and thorough check-ins to keep things in order and operating at a healthy and sustainable capacity. We can tune into our own energies and dig into the depths of the darkest backroom in search of what's not working. We're not designed to be or remain creatively and spiritually constipated. We are intended to flow with our best selves. When we get better at discerning our motives, the more we can enjoy what we do and how, whenever and wherever we do it.

We can also recognize and accept the dualities of where we are and where we may want to be. We will get there. In the meantime, we can drop the mental tug of war and give thanks for the beautiful gift that we all have, right *now* . . . and now . . . and now—the gift to simply *be*. *Be* the Shopkeeper, the business owner, the parent, the friend, the partner, the leader, the person that you already are. Give yourself grace now and as you grow. We don't have to fight ourselves and our circumstances so much.

I learned all the above the hard way. My time as a Shopkeeper was meant to open me up to lifelong lessons, spur professional and spiritual growth, and nurture my passions while fostering community in the place that I called home. All in all, a success.

The success of your Shopkeeper Dream is yours to define from the beginning of your journey to wherever it takes you. Along the road remember this: When we lead with our heartset, our lives can change and evolve with the truest intentions and clarity in direction. We can live our dreams and navigate anything with a curious mind, an open heart, and a trusty personal inventory sheet. We get to choose how we experience our everyday.

AFTERWORD

My biggest challenges as a Shopkeeper, as shared in this book, had to do with the realization and awareness of my personal emotions, energies, and their effects on those around me, my business, and myself.

As I entered the final editing stages of OPEN, I learned that I have premenstrual dysphoric disorder (PMDD). It was a profound shock, then relief, and has brought a new understanding to the stories you have read.

PMDD is like premenstrual syndrome (PMS) on steroids, but it's not just hormonal; it's how the brain processes the monthly hormonal changes. The International Association for Premenstrual Disorders (IAPMD) states that *PMDD is a severe negative reaction in the brain to the natural rise and fall of estrogen and progesterone.*

I knew that something was off for a long time, but I made excuses for not digging deeper. Every month, I accepted my inevitable monthly symptoms, telling myself, *Here we go again. Let's all brace ourselves*, as if my norm was well, normal. The self-loathing, erratic, and irritable moods, and depressive states I have experienced like clockwork every two to three weeks since my first daughter was born have intensified year after year. No matter the tools I had in those moments, I needed so much more support.

The point came when I hit rock bottom and immediately sought help from a general practitioner, a naturopath, and a therapist. Thanks to them and to my new sense of urgency, I now have solutions, or rather, new tools to work through the moments when I am most vulnerable. My world has forever changed, knowing that I can manage my cyclical experiences and, for the most part, keep symptoms at bay. Symptoms that when out in full force, impacted my days and relationships for the worse.

I am sharing all this because it's a huge part of the ongoing journey of taking personal inventory in every season of life, often and honestly. PMDD has played a huge role in my life, long before I had a name for it, and many of the stories in this book were surely impacted by the disorder.

For anyone who might have a deeper issue like me, know you are not alone. I know how isolating it can be when managing personal emotions and energies feels beyond your control—because they literally are. Until you learn more and build your own set of tools.

A diagnosis during my shopkeeping days would have been life-changing, but I suppose that in some ways, the way it played out is fitting for this book; a reminder to stay curious about what makes us tick, dim, glow, and burn out—and take action accordingly. A reminder to give ourselves grace as we evolve and live the *YES* out of life.

Learn more at iapmd.org

ACKNOWLEDGMENTS

Thank you to my editor, Sara, for enthusiastically guiding me to the finish line. You held my hand just enough to push me and this book to be that much better. Thank you to Jenna, for caring for every word, comma, period, and dotted *i* for the final polish. Thank you to Tess, for the thoughtful book design inside and out—your perspective and know-how proved to be invaluable. And many thanks to Jessie, who edited my very first and very rough draft years prior. Your loving touch set me on the right path.

Thank you to the PofR community of customers, artists, designers, sales reps, business owners, and friends who brought so much joy into my life. For five years, your daily support and shared enthusiasm were a gift that I continue to cherish. So much of this book is a love note to you. And of course, Leslie, Amanda, Katie, Anissa, and Jess—you made the dream work by choosing to work with me. Thank you always and forever.

Thank you to all the independent Shopkeepers I connected and shared stories with along the way. You're an inspiration to me and an example of what it means to build and live out your dream. You make our communities so much brighter.

Thank you to friends who were privy to this book for months or years, checking in and cheering for me. Your curiosity and support are appreciated more than you'll ever know. Thank you for believing in me across all my creations.

Gracias a mi familia, my mom, dad, and sister. You are the backbone of my world, and no words can describe how much you lift me up every day. Thank you for everything, always.

Thank you to my love, my husband, the solid rock to my La Niña winds—you see and love me through all the seasons. I am forever grateful for the life we've created together and the adventures yet to come.

To my two daughters, thank you for choosing me to be your mama. You motivate me to chase my dreams so that you may do the same. I love watching you both light up.

RESOURCES

Download a FREE Walk-In Sheet template and explore more templates available for purchase:

Read and subscribe to the OPEN for Growith Substack:

NOTES

i. Mojica, Luis, host, "How Trauma Affects Your Business," Holistic Life Navigation (podcast), March 5, 2021, accessed September 10, 2023, https://www.buzzsprout.com/278649/7941085-ep-37-how-trauma-affects-your-business-holly-howard-consultant.

ii. Larson, Brie, director. *Unicorn Store*. 51 Entertainment, 2017. 92 min.

iii. Kurcinka, Mary S. 2016. *Raising Your Spirited Child*. 3rd ed. HarperCollins.

iv. Tolle, Eckhart, "A New Earth: The Discovery of Inner Space (Chapter 8)," Essential Teachings (podcast), March 10, 2019, accessed September 10, 2023, https://podcasts.apple.com/us/podcast/a-new-earth-the-discovery-of-inner-space-chapter-8/id1458654443?i=1000434071526.

v. Kuzminski, Kevin. "Cheap Books, Generous Donations: Owner of Raleigh Bookstore Finds Ways to Give." WRAL News. June 27, 2021. https://www.wral.com/cheap-books-generous-donations-owner-of-raleigh-bookstore-finds-ways-to-give-back/19742108/.

ABOUT THE AUTHOR

Ana Maria Muñoz is a creative marketing consultant, writer, and mentor who believes that everything is an experience and every touchpoint counts. A former shopkeeper with over two decades of retail experience, she works with entrepreneurs and business leaders to reignite their spark for connecting with customers and themselves.

Ana Maria serves as a retail mentor and workshop facilitator with the Polaris Business Centre in South Australia and has spoken at Life In Style and Reed Gift Fairs. Her work has been featured in *Design Milk*, *Tastemade Home*, and numerous publications worldwide.

Raised in Los Angeles and shaped by years living in London, Kuala Lumpur, and Raleigh, Ana Maria draws on her cross-cultural experiences to connect the dots for personal and collective growth. She lives in Adelaide, South Australia, with her husband, two daughters, and Golden Retriever Lab. When she's not in mom-mode or writing for her Substacks *AM Notes* and *OPEN for Growth*, she's chasing her Y.E.S. (Your Energetic Spark™) by learning to DJ. OPEN is Ana Maria's first book.

anamariamunoz.com

www.ingramcontent.com/pod-product-compliance
Lightning Source LLC
Chambersburg PA
CBHW031242290426
44109CB00012B/398